AF552865

Curriculum for Disaster Preparedness

Dr. A. Rama Krishna
M.Sc., M.Ed., M.Phil., Ph.D.
Associate Professor
Department of Education
Osmania University
Hyderabad 500007

Editors

Dr. M. Sree Rama Murthy
Former Dean, Faculty of Education
Osmania University
Hyderabad 500007

Dr. Digumarti Bhaskara Rao
M.Sc., M.A., M.A., M.Ed., Ph.D.
Reader
R.V.R. College of Education
Srinivasa Nagar Colony
Guntur–522006
Andhra Pradesh (India)
&
Member, Board of Studies in Education
Acharya Nagarjuna University
Nagarjuna Nagar–522510
Andhra Pradesh

DISCOVERY PUBLISHING HOUSE
NEW DELHI

Reprinted - 2019

First Published - 2006

ISBN: 978-81-8356-076-4

Curriculum for Disaster Preparedness

Published by:
DISCOVERY PUBLISHING HOUSE PVT. LTD.
4383/4B, Ansari Road, Darya Ganj
New Delhi-110 002 (India)
Phone: +91-11-23279245, 23253475; 43596065
E-mail: discoverybooksindia@gmail.com
discoverypublishinghouse@gmail.com
web: www.discoverypublishinggroup.com

Printed at:
Infinity Imaging Systems
Delhi

Dedicated

to

the personnel and public

who

render services

to

the disaster victims

PREFACE

Disasters cause much damage to mankind. They occur unnoticingly and the result could be great human and animal loss alongwith changes in environment. Knowing the very role of disaster management several countries have established disaster management centers. They also have developed and are practising suitable curriculum for disaster preparedness. This book is an attempt to identify certain curricular issues made available for disaster preparedness.

The author is thankful to Prof. Sree Rama Murthy, Dr. D. Bhaskara Rao and Mr. Tilak Wasan, who are instrumental in preparing and publishing this book on curriculum for disaster preparedness.

Department of Education
Osmania University
Hyderabad–500007
Andhra Pradesh

Rama Krishna

CONTENTS

1

INTRODUCTION

Introduction

Seldom does a month go by without a major catastrophe occurring somewhere in the world with a consequent tragic toll of death, injury and property damage.

In India, out of the 32 States/Union Territories, 24 States are vulnerable for drought, flood, cyclone and earthquake. These emergency situations kill thousands of people every year and cause huge economic losses. The money diverted for relief work hinders other development in the State. Economists, social scientists and developmental activity planners are evaluating the possible benefits of laying emphasis on prevention as against recovery on development and long-term national economic gains.

As a citizen one should be aware of hazards and potential disasters, how and when they are likely to occur and problems which may result and how to cope with their effects. There is information on survival and property protection which deals with what to do before, during and after the impact of that particular hazard and thereby reduce the possibility of it becoming a disaster.

If status quo of the physical systems or processes is preserved-which are said to be governed by the so-called laws of nature-then no disaster can be triggered off. Once this state of stability breaks down, catastrophic results begin to occur.

The event leads to a disaster when

(a) it is extreme in magnitude,

(b) the population is very great, or

(c) the human – use system is particularly vulnerable.

Disaster is an event either man-made or natural, sudden or progressive in occurrence, the impact of which is such that the affected communities must respond through measures which exceed their own immediate capabilities (Activity Report, 1992).

Hazard and Disaster

A hazard is a physical phenomenon which can be potentially dangerous to life and property. Whereas a disaster occurs when a hazard mechanism actually damages people, property and crops.

Disasters occur as certain communities or groups are forced to settle in areas susceptible to the impact of geo-physical features such as a raging river or a volcanic eruption. The Figure 1.1 illustrates this combination of opposing forces. Vulnerability is seen as the progression of three stages:

1. Underlying causes: a deep-rooted set of factors within a society which together forms and maintains vulnerability.

2. Dynamic pressures: a translating process that channels the effects of a negative cause into unsafe conditions; this process may be due to lack of basic services or provision or it may result from a series of macro-forces.

3. Unsafe conditions: the vulnerable context where people and property are exposed to the risk of disaster; the fragile physical environment is one element; other factors include an unstable economy and low income levels.

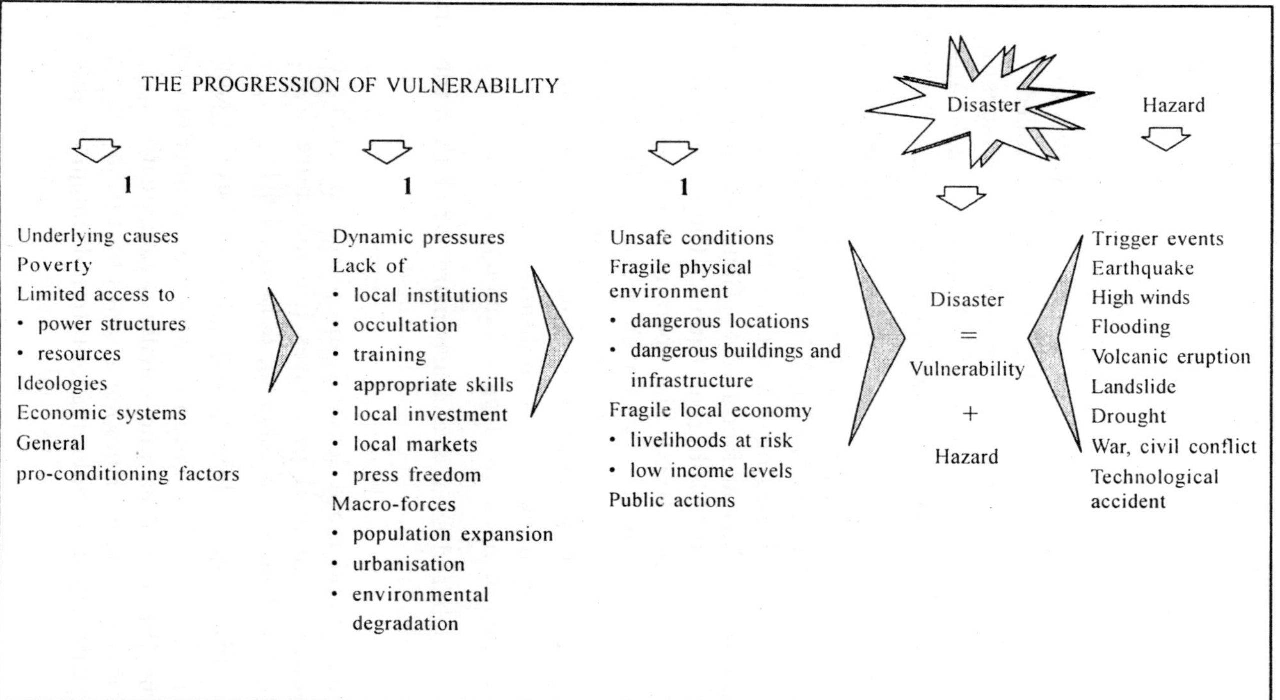

Figure 1.1: The Disaster Crunch Model (Blaike, et. al. 1994)

Frequency of Disasters

All disasters, natural or man-made, have one thing in common: their capacity to maim, cause unmentionable misery, and loss of property and lives. However, THE WORLD DISASTER REPORT, 1994, published by the International Federation of Red Cross and Red Crescent Societies, suggests that the havoc can be controlled. Often, it is the improper dissemination or censorship of information by the powers-that-be which exacerbates the suffering of the people (Down To Earth, August 31, 1994).

About 95% of lives lost in disasters every year occur in developing countries and the economic loss in terms of percentage of Gross National Product (GNP at factor cost is computed by adding net income from abroad to Gross Domestic Product at factor cost – General Studies Manual, 1998) is 20 to 30% higher than in the developed world (Activity Report, 1992). Sixty percent of the world's major disasters occur in the Asia-Pacific region, and countries that are at greater risk – due to population increases and vulnerability because of their physical environment - have placed a very high priority on disaster management and the mitigation of hazards (Jeggle, January, 1994).

Urbanised areas are clearly more at risk than the rural open countryside because potentially large numbers of fatalities can result during a disaster. As the population increases and more demands are placed on earth's limited resources, natural processes become more serious as potential disasters (Pickering & Lewis, 1994).

The countries in Asia and the Pacific are highly disaster prone. Among the top-ten countries by number of disasters (1966-1990) in Asia and Pacific region, in the industrial countries category Hongkong ranks first with 220 while in the category of developing countries Philippines tops with 272 and is followed by India with 216 (Activity Report, 1992).

In the period between 1960 and 1980, the frequency of major natural disasters has increased 5 times. Since 1990, there occurred 2,115 disasters, of which 770 were cyclones, 675 floods, 375 earthquakes, 225 drought and 70 volcanic eruptions (Activity Report, 1992).

On an average, disasters killed more than 1.2 lakh people and affected more than 135.5 million people between 1971 – 1995 every year. Floods killed the maximum number of people in Asia, particularly China and Bangladesh. In Africa, drought and famine continued to dominate, accounting for almost one-third of the disaster events. Ethiopia and Sudan were the worst-hit (Activity Report, 1992).

The number and percentage of disasters with natural trigger in 1996 is given in table 1.1.

Table 1.1: Disasters with natural trigger—1996 (Down to Earth, October 31, 1997)

Type of disaster	*Number*	*Percentage*
Drought & famine	4	2.2%
Earthquake	12	6.7%
Flood	65	36.1%
Landslide	14	7.8%
High wind	43	23.9%
Volcano	4	2.2%
Other	38	21.1%

Table 1.1 reveals that almost sixty percent of disasters around the world were due to high winds and floods.

The number and percentage of disasters with natural trigger in 1971-95, is shown in table 1.2.

The comparison of Tables 1.1 and 1.2 shows that although disasters in 1996 decreased by fifteen percent as

Table 1.2: Disasters with a natural trigger, 1971 – 95 (Down To Earth, October 31, 1997)

Type of disaster	*Number*	*Percentage*
Drought & famine	469	9.0%
Earthquake	678	12.9%
Flood	1,508	28.8%
Landslide	232	4.4%
High wind	1,650	31.5%
Volcano	110	2.1%
Other	593	11.3%

compared to 1995, the number of people affected by them went up by six percent.

The number of disasters triggered by natural causes according to their region and type in 1996 is shown in table 1.3.

Table 1.3: Number of disasters triggered by natural causes, by region and type—1996 (The World Disaster Report, 1997)

Type	*Africa*	*America*	*Asia*	*Europe*	*Oceania*	*Total*
Drought & Famine	3	1	0	0	0	4
Volcano	0	2	0	1	1	4
High wind	2	16	22	2	1	43
Landslide	1	5	4	2	2	14
Flood	14	17	23	9	2	65
Earthquake	0	4	6	2	0	12
Other	18	1	16	3	0	38
Total	38	46	71	19	6	180

(Other – Cold wave, Heat wave, Insect infestation, Tsunami)

Table 1.3 reveals that the maximum number of disasters were floods with 65 in number followed by high winds which were 43.

Nature of Disaster Prevention

In the past, there was a one-way relationship when only natural hazards had an impact on human society and caused disasters. People tried to adjust with nature by keeping away from disaster prone areas and at the same time accepting benefits from nature. Natural hazards such as earthquake and volcanic eruption still have a one-way relationship as they cannot be prevented from occurring, although responses to them have greatly improved.

But, in recent years, human activities have been interfering with nature and inducing the natural phenomena to cause disasters in new areas and with increasing severity in existing disaster-prone areas. Therefore, one-way relationship between natural hazards and human activities of the past has now changed into a two-way relationship in which human activities have considerable impact on natural phenomena causing disasters. These aspects are represented in figure 1.2.

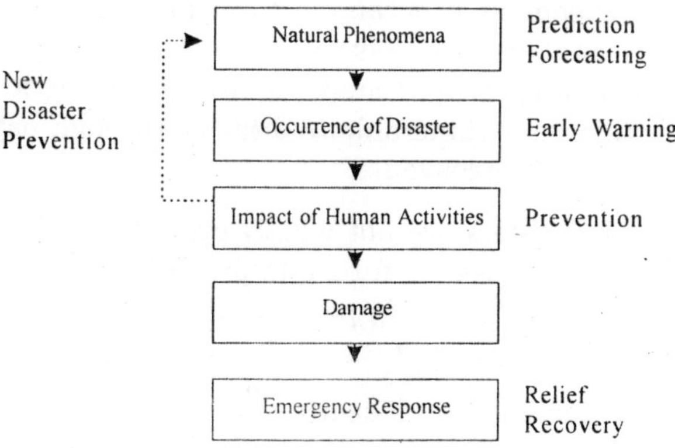

Figure 1.2: Traditional Disaster Prevention (Disaster Management and Regional Development Planning with People's Participation, 1990).

The traditional concept of disaster prevention, which impedes the one-way flow from natural phenomena to human activities, is to minimise impact upon to human activities by natural phenomena. However, human activities lately have been affecting natural environment and as a result damage has been far more serious. Thus, a new concept of two-directional disaster prevention is needed, because traditional one-way disaster management concept has serious limitations.

During disasters there will be a delay, before help arrives. Therefore initially, self-help is essential and depends upon having a prepared community – that is a community which:

(a) is alert, informed and actively aware;

(b) has an active and involved local government; and

(c) has agreed and co-ordinated arrangements for disaster prevention, preparedness, response and recovery (Hazards, Disasters and Survival, 1992).

In a disaster prone country, there should not be any complacency in preparedness. People's awareness should be kept alive all the time through effective publicity. The disaster management programme covering both structural and non-structural measures, though complex and expensive, should be pursued vigorously in regions or countries which are vulnerable to disaster through national and international endeavours.

Natural disasters are not wholly preventable. It is not possible in the foreseeable future to prevent disasters from occurring. Therefore, it is imperative that emphasis is laid on managing and reducing its effects (Quarantelli, 1991).

A good percentage of death and destruction brought about by disaster especially those due to natural causes could have been prevented if populace had known what to do to protect themselves.

Disaster Management

The fact that disasters do occur only when the effective forces of natural phenomena become unmanageable suggests the need for every member of the community to be educated in disaster management.

There is a strong need to strengthen the resilience and self confidence of local communities to cope with natural disasters through recognition and propagation of their traditional knowledge, practices and values as part of development activities.

Greater awareness and information dissemination are necessary in the field of disaster management. Some of the issues regarding disaster management should be in the syllabi of schools, colleges and universities. There is a consensus that disaster management should be included in the development planning.

Disaster management encompasses a variety of activities like mitigation, preparedness, activity during the event, relief and restoration of structures. While the benefits of preparedness are short-term, the investment can save lives, and money spent on preparedness will help to reduce the incidence of suffering following the disaster and can shorten the recovery time.

Given the acute resource limitations that prevail throughout the Third World, the more realistic term 'mitigation' has replaced 'prevention' in recent years. 'Mitigation' can be defined in an abbreviated form as 'actions taken to reduce damage and loss'. There is a series of distinct ways in which this can take place, and risk-reduction typologies abound (Burton, et. al. 1978). These include measures to reduce the physical hazard, to provide structural and non-structural mitigation (including specialised agricultural mitigation measures), and to increase preparedness.

A detailed description of the various aspects of disaster management is represented in figure 1.3.

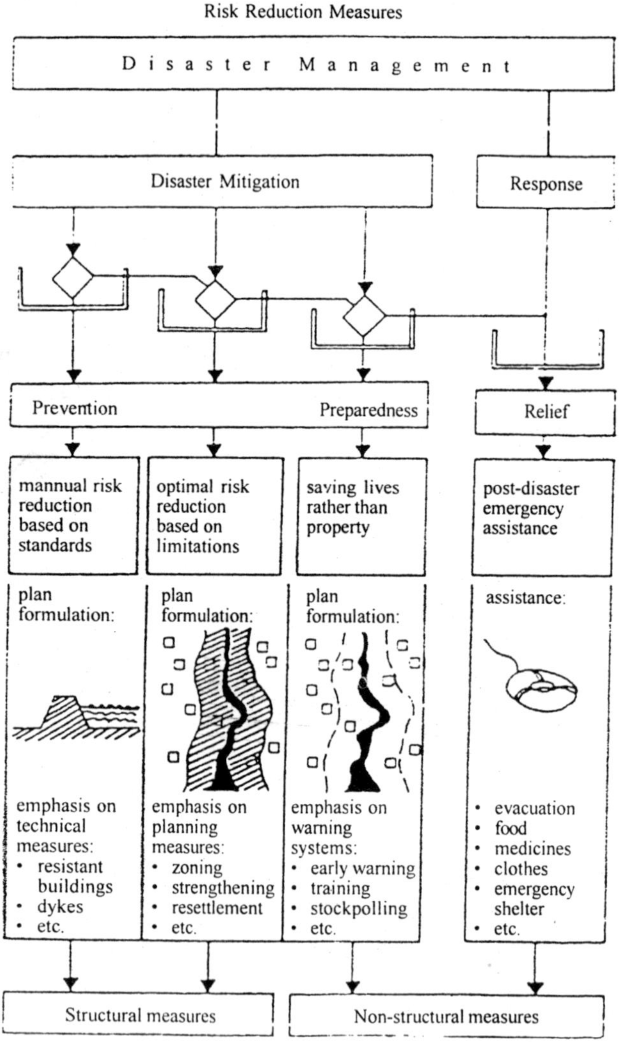

Risk Reduction Measures

Figure 1.3: Risk Reduction Measures (Weirsing, 1995)

As shown in figure 1.3, among the non-structural measures forecasting, preparedness, land occupation and agricultural practices are important.

After a disaster, a large number of volunteers with high motivation, but low role competence, attempt uncordinated rescue operations. Naturally such attempts are not effective and will also lead to wastage of precious resources and – more importantly, time. Such a situation can be prevented if the response pattern of these well meaning individuals/agencies are trained for effective co-ordination in such times.

The structural aspect of disaster management should also be covered and incorporated in the training course so that the personnel involved in disaster management are confident of managing and handling disasters efficiently.

According to Perry & Meredith (1978), short-term pre-impact evacuation has been termed preventive; long-term pre-impact evacuation can be described as protective; short-term post-impact withdrawal involves rescue; and long-term post-impact evacuation is linked to reconstruction.

The main obstacle is not warning or disaster preparedness but rather motivating people to heed the warning and evacuate the disaster-prone areas. Human behaviour and action are cardinal in the 'disaster cycle'. having elements such as emergency response, rehabilitation, reconstruction, prevention and preparedness. Failure to cope with natural calamities is identified as a disaster, threat or hazard by the affected people rather than the calamity itself.

Role of Education

Prevention or at least diminution of the disaster effects can be achieved by education.

Education and training of general public and especially the community leaders in disaster management is necessary. In disaster-prone countries, basic disaster management procedure may be included in the educational texts from primary to high school level.

Education teaches the basis of everything for later life. This is the "banking" approach to education alluded to by educators such as Friere (1972). Basically, it suggests that a front end investment will bring later rewards. It is an approach that is common to many training courses including those concerned with disaster preparedness.

The most important item of planning for disaster is education of the general public to eliminate superstitions and ignorance which can augment the destructive effects of a disaster. This will prepare the people to take suitable preventive action.

Converting disaster victims into potential helping resources should involve public education, training, techniques, etc.

Education in disaster prevention measures should begin at school by informing pupils about disaster effects and methods of protection against disaster. The education of the person can begin at the primary school level.

According to Lystad (1987) psychological reactions to disaster may be specific to the age of the victim. In this respect, children are often particularly vulnerable. Especially in the age group 6-12 years, children are unable to understand and rationalise the event. They may suffer from confusion, depression fears about their own safety, fighting, headaches or other physical complaints, inability to concentrate, poor performance and withdrawal from peers.

Children are vulnerable to the same stresses as the adult population, with additional complications that they are less able to articulate their feelings, and may be affected adversely by family disharmony which often occurs after disaster (Powell and Penwick, 1983). It has also been widely observed that parents tend to deny children's problems (Burke et al., 1982), and that intervention can be offered most appropriately in a school context (Klingman, 1988).

Initiatives such as the working group set up in Bradford to consider the needs of children (Harrison, 1987c) are a necessary contribution to knowledge in this area.

The educational system in particular, including primary and adult education activities, should be used for educating people about disasters.

The role of schools as basic resources in the training of disaster management is recognised. Hence, specific training programmes and measures should be undertaken to equip schools with disaster management training capabilities, e.g. the teachers at the primary school levels should be trained in disaster preparedness and disaster prevention measures as well as environmental protection measures so that they can inculcate the right ideas and attitudes in the children.

If education and training programme are to be successful, curricular instructional materials, etc., need to be prepared rationally. Curriculum development can hardly be put in straight jacket format. Unlike the traditional procedures there is a need to be wide-awake to the questions about the subject matter of learning, target groups, and learning media. An appropriate pedagogy for educating the community has to be developed and as one involved in education, few basic questions related to teaching learning structure need to be raised such as who needs to learn, how it could be learnt and what needs to be learnt (Chaudhuri, 1992).

The ultimate objective of the training module is not only to equip the people in facing and mitigating disaster but also to give them moral and mental strength to face disaster without feeling helpless.

A more systematic training module based upon their special role in disaster management, in India, still needs to be evolved (Singh, 1992). Hence, the present work entitled, "Curriculum for Disaster Preparedness" has been taken up.

The details of the problem and the manner in which it has been worked out i.e., operational definitions, objectives, review of related literature, hypotheses, limitations, development of the questionnaire, analysis of data, inferences and suggestions of the study are discussed in the subsequent chapters.

2

THE PROBLEM

The statement of the problem, context and significance of the topic, operational definitions, objectives of the study, review of related literature, hypotheses and limitations of the study are discussed in this chapter.

Statement of the Problem

The broad subject area chosen by the investigator is disaster management. The specific aspect of the present study is the development of a curriculum for preparing the children to face disaster situations. The problem has been worded as "Curriculum for Disaster Preparedness".

Context and Significance of the Topic

When fire broke out in the "Escuela Republic de Haiti", an elementary school in Costa Rica, 900 pupils were in their classrooms. Four minutes later, all the students and their teachers were safely outside the building. By the time the fire fighters arrived, three classrooms, the kitchen and the cafeteria of the school had been completely destroyed, but there were no human losses. The pupils of the 'Escuela' had taken part in safety drills and evacuation exercises regularly as part of an international programme by "Partners of the Americas" launched in the early 1990s. The programme taught young people simple protective measures against natural and man-made disasters. When the alarm bell went off, they knew how to proceed, and no one was hurt (IDNDR, Fact Sheet Series No.1. 11 Oct., 1995).

In another instance, a twelve year old boy saved seven of his family members who were buried under the debris, in an earthquake that shook Latur, Maharashtra in September, 1993.

Those usually most affected by natural and other disasters are the poor and socially disadvantaged groups in developing countries as they are least equipped to cope with them. They try to overcome the negative effects usually through traditional unscientific approaches resulting in more harm rather than help that is possible with a scientific approach.

It would be hardly prudent to let a disaster play havoc and then look for relief coming from donors. One should have prior knowledge and preparation to tackle disaster havoc, if they occur.

The most important aspect of preparedness is to influence immediate decisions which the individuals have to take once the event occurs. At this juncture it is important that one does not have to think about what to do and how to do, because the prepared individual can use the resources, physical, material or psychological immediately. This would help to minimise the losses or damages.

One can reduce the effects of disasters, if one is aware, one shares and prepares the details of which are given below:

Be aware—know the area's history. Ask the family friends if they experienced disasters. Learn about weather patterns, movements within the earth, and how they affect the environment.

Share—Use drawings, school events, even newspapers, radio or television to tell the community information gathered.

Prepare—Find out what warning announcements mean. Find safe places to go. Do drills. Make survival kit, etc.

Operational Definitions

In order to facilitate a clear perspective, it is preferred to provide the operational definitions of the words incorporated in the problem. They are explained in the following paragraphs:

Curriculum

A curriculum is a specification of content and principles to be investigated within classroom realities. The Primary School curriculum of Classes I, II & III are considered for the study.

Disaster

Sheehan and Hewitt (1967) defined disasters as situations which satisfy at least one of the following conditions:

(a) at least $ 10,00,000 damage or

(b) at least 100 dead or

(c) at least 100 injured.

Disasters come in all shapes and sizes. They can occur anywhere and they are unpredictable to a large extent—disasters can occur at any hour of the day or night (Hazards, Disasters and Survival, 1992). Disasters can vary from each other in the following ways:

Cause—They can be natural, or man-made (e.g. flood/transport accidents);

Frequency—Some occur more often than others (e.g. bushfire/earthquakes);

Duration—Some may be of limited duration, others may go on for quite long periods of time (e.g. earthquakes/droughts);

Speed of onset—Some happen very quickly, while with others there is a warning period of perhaps hours or days (e.g. bushfire/cyclone).

Scope of impact—Some disasters may affect a relatively small area, and others may affect whole countries (e.g. tornado/famine);

Destructive potential—Varies enormously with the types of hazards (e.g. landslide/cyclone);

Predictability—Some hazards follow certain patterns, and others do not (e.g. floods/toxic emission);

Controllability—With some disasters man is totally helpless and must let them run their course, while in others he can do something to lessen the impact even if he cannot prevent them from occurring (e.g. volcanoes/bushfires).

Disaster Preparedness

Disaster preparedness may be described as an ability to respond to a disaster situation to minimise loss of life and damage, and to organise and facilitate timely and effective rescue, relief and rehabilitation. It is concerned with forecasting and warning; education and training of the population; organisation and management of disaster situations (Cuny, 1983).

Behaviour

'Behaviour' covers everything children do and is one of the principal means by which one can recognise what they are thinking, feeling and experiencing. Behaviour is linked to their stage of development, personality and capacity to cope (Maureen & Maureen, 1990). Thus, the term behaviour is hard to define and harder to comprehend. To attempt an all encompassing definition of behaviour is beyond the scope of the present study. Therefore, an attempt has been made to comprehend behaviour by means of a set of behavioural traits.

Objectives of the Study

In view of the above discussion, the investigator has formulated the following objectives for the study:

1. To list out the disasters that occur in India with a natural trigger.
2. To establish behavioural traits essential to meet natural disaster situations.
3. To suggest the curricular activities at primary school level for developing the behavioural traits essential to meet the disaster situations.
4. To incorporate the developed activities in the existing primary school curriculum.

Review of Related Literature

The studies related to the problem "Curriculum for Disaster Preparedness" were organised into four categories, namely, Curriculum and related issues, Disaster Preparedness, Training and skills, and Disaster Management in India. These aspects are represented in the figure shown below:

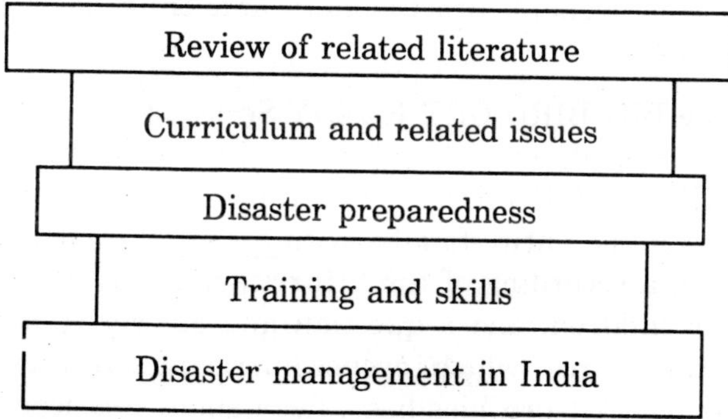

The review in this section covers the books, children television workshop projects, documents, techniques, nature of material, models of learning, curriculum and activities.

The book—Emergency/Disaster Planning For Principals (1992)—is suitable for use by pre-schools, kindergartens/ infants, primary and secondary schools. It describes that:

(a) Prevention/Preparedness measures aim to reduce the likelihood of an emergency occurring by carrying out activities which remove or minimise potential risks.

(b) Response is the activity which is carried out immediately an emergency occurs and lasts until the risks to personal safety and/or property has been removed.

(c) In general, the teaching staff normally retains responsibility for their students. The book discusses what the teachers are expected to do during an emergency.

The Natural Hazard Project (Organisation of American States, 1984) is the first Children Television Workshop Project to reach parents, pre-schoolers and older children. The formative research for the Natural Hazard Project included an extensive literature search, an informal investigation with children and adults around the country, a two-day seminar and a series of discussions with natural hazard researchers, practitioners and child development specialists.

The BIG BIRD GET READY Series of family kits are being developed, one for each natural hazard. The first kit, BIG BIRD GET READY for hurricanes, includes a 16 page booklet for the entire family (with essential information in Spanish), a recording of the "Hurricane Blues", a song for younger children, and a question and answer game called "Hurricane Force" which teaches hurricane safety, facts and science. The kit provides basic facts about hurricanes, tips about what to do long before, during and after a hurricane, and suggestions for putting together a family safety plan.

The relevant inferences drawn from the above study are:

(a) Most children can cope with change, if they are prepared for it.

(b) Children's responses depend on those of the adults around them.

(c) People can learn to be prepared for natural hazards.

(d) Just after a natural hazard occurs, people's interest is temporarily heightened. This is the 'Teachable Moment'.

(e) Information designed for children (and adults) should progress from the simple and familiar to the more complex.

The American Red Cross Disaster Community Education Programme – Chapter Activities in Disaster Community Education: A Resource Guide (American Red Cross 1986) documents 65 chapter educational activities in over 40 chapters. The Resource Guide demonstrates that there are dozens of different strategies chapters have used to meet specific community disaster education needs. It is a compilation of chapter experiences and strategies grouped according to similar approaches taken by other chapters.

According to Gardiner (1990) simulation techniques such as modelling and video can be used to persuade the public, without causing the confusion, distress and other intangible damage wrought by an actual flood event.

Handmer and Penning-Rowsell (1990) recommended that:

(a) risk communication messages should deal with affective and emotional aspects, and

(b) in many cases material should be prepared in advance so that it is ready for immediate distribution when the time is appropriate, i.e., at the 'teachable moment'.

For improving the behaviour of the child according to behaviourists appropriate response would be brought about through reinforcement, either positive or negative, or through punishment (Wilson, 1990). But, Bandura and Walters (1963) emphasised the importance of role modelling, suggesting that most of our meaningful learning is achieved through example, more correctly termed imitation (or observational learning). This involves acquiring appropriate responses as a result of seeing a model.

On one hand, the neo-behaviourists developed the concept of learned helplessness which essentially implies that when someone is unable to overcome a repeated negative situation, behaviour will adjust so that there is no longer any desire to avoid the situation. While on the other, Knowles (1970, 1984) recognised that the best time for learning is when the need to know is present. Thus, ideally it would be more productive to target educational programmes towards those who need to know, such as intending or recent residents in a floodplain, than simply to go for a blanket approach.

According to instructional theorists learning involves physical skills, mental skills and attitudes, and that there are various levels of learning within each domain. Thus, while transferring various facts or knowledge about say, taking out flood insurance, this may be wasted if attention is not paid to higher level cognitive processes, or to the attitudinal or emotional aspects such as its value or its sense of responsibility. These aspects (Blooms Taxonomy of Educational Objectives) are represented in the following figure:

	PSYCHO-MOTOR	COGNITIVE	AFFECTIVE
Lower Level Learning	Imitation	Knowledge	Receiving
	Manipulation	Comprehension	Responding
	Precision	Application	Valuing
	Articulation	Analysis	Organising
	Naturalisation	Synthesis	Characterising
Higher Level Learning			Evaluation

The cognitivists developed models based on.the intellectual processes involved in learning and the influence of organisation, decision-making, information processing and forgetting. Bruner (1965, 1966, 1974) and Ausubel (1963, 1968) stressed the need to develop concepts as an aid to both memory and to choices of action rather than simply transmitting facts. If, for example, to teach fire fighters about safety procedures in fires, one could take either of the two approaches. One approach involves teaching safety as a set of procedures to be followed, and another teaching it in the context of the concept of fire behaviour. According to Bruner and Ausubel, the latter is a better approach. Although simply teaching procedures may be satisfactory in certain circumstances, should unexpected circumstances develop the procedures would not fit the new situation. Someone who has the broader concept would be more likely to use adaptive behaviour.

On the contrary, Rogers (1951, 1969) views education as facilitative rather than pedagogical, and takes the philosophical position that personal feelings ought to be respected, and that self-determination is everyone's right. Roger's perspective is suitable for non-formal models of education.

School children should be introduced to simple mitigation measures in the context of environmental studies, natural sciences, or geography classes. Fiji and the Phillipines have developed appropriate curricula and materials to support such teaching programmes, which may serve other countries in the Asian and Pacific region in the development of their own teaching programmes (Disaster Mitigation in Asia and the Pacific, 1991).

The four blocks suggested by Goutam. P.R. (1992) consists of geography and environment, human activities, social and economic status of people, and knowledge of lifelines (transportation and energy) in Block I; knowledge of disaster including past history, causes and effects and various factors affecting them in Block II; preparedness and preventive measures, rescue and relief operations and rehabilitation in Block III; and the integration of disaster mitigation measures in the hill area development planning in Block IV has covered the broad range of subject matters pertaining to the disaster management needs of the country.

Further, he concluded that training curriculum structured around the disaster of today will help to save many more lives and properties in the disaster next year.

Hazard-wise, Emergency Management Australia (1995) provides the teacher with a ready-to-use classroom resource which covers many aspects of major natural hazards and disasters. Through a series of exercises, students are stimulated to investigate the causes and effects of hazards and the way in which people can respond effectively to them. Each section contains activities designed to arouse greater interest in the topic such as crossword puzzles, research activities and role play exercises.

China has developed mass disaster education and training for government officials (Jingshen & Gang, 1992).

A pedagogical framework for disaster studies at the level of adult education is presented by Alexander (1991).

An ATLAS of the natural disaster in Asia to facilitate study of the origin and development as well as distribution factors of various disasters in reduction and prevention should be prepared which will

(a) promote research of the disaster causes, principles and mechanism, and study of the natural disaster prevention and control, and

(b) provide theoretical and scientific bases for the disaster prevention, reduction, control and decision-making (Development of Modules for Training on Integrated approach to Disaster Management and Regional/Rural Development Planning, 1992, p.88).

"Learning about Natural Disasters - Games and projects for you and your friends" (Stop disasters/IDNDR, 1995) provides activities of the following kinds:

(a) DRAWING A MAP OF YOUR COMMUNITY

i. Spotting Danger and taking action

ii. Grandma, do you remember...?

iii. Draw Risk and resource symbols

(b) DRAWING A MAP OF YOUR COMMUNITY:

i. Hunt for hazards and find ways to avoid them

ii. Take action

iii. Enter the community map contest

iv. Save natalie: The Preparedness Game

(c) COMMUNICATING THROUGH ART:

i. Draw a recent disaster

ii. Draw a disaster that could happen to your community

iii. Draw how to be safe

(d) RAISING AWARENESS IN YOUR COMMUNITY:

i. Be a reporter

ii. Use books, magazines or newspapers

iii. Using radio

(e) REPORTING TO YOUR COMMUNITY:

i. Putting it all together.

Earthquake Safety - Activities for Children describes - "What happens during an earthquake?" (IDNDR, Fact Sheet Series No.1, 11, Oct., 1995).

According to Sinha (1992)

1. A Curriculum of education on natural disasters which comprises of its development through training, preparation of instructional materials, development of teaching aids and enrichment materials at different levels is yet to be developed. The only organisation which has made an initiative in this direction is Pan-African Centre for Emergency Preparedness and Response under the auspices of the World Health Organisation. Some of its publications in this direction are really useful not only for general purpose but also for training programmes for trainers.

2. The formal system like that of the universities has to participate in building up a curriculum on natural disasters. Professional institutions and non-governmental organisations should be supported to augment activities in appraising people, say, on community preparedness so that it acquires a conceptually acceptable status and perhaps, respectability, if these activities are imparted by management institutes/departments, education and training departments of universities or similar autonomous bodies.

Long-term education programmes are necessary to prevent the recurrence of similar disasters from the same hazard (Disaster Mitigation in Asia and the Pacific, 1991).

Valussi (1984) examined the needs for a hazard and risk education curriculum in the seismic areas of Italy on the basis that school can play an important role in raising community consciousness about hazard and risk. He concluded that students had a limited perception of the hazards which faced them and attributed this to lack of educational action.

Further he stressed that risk education must take a contextual approach in school curriculum, rather than form its own distinct set of curriculum or content. There is already a large number of risk related "curricula", such as road safety, health, drugs and so on, with which such a curriculum would need to compete for school curriculum time. Unless risk and hazard education material contributes to existing school-based curriculum goals, it is likely to be ignored by the majority of teachers as peripheral, irrelevant or of lesser importance.

Disaster Preparedness

This section of the review provides insights into the importance, approach, nature, problems and suggestions – of the disaster preparedness programmes.

When faced with an uncertain outcome people tend to adopt the behaviour they believe likely to produce the least negative outcome. Further, it is difficult to predict the way people will react in a major emergency situation, but knowledge of the correct procedure will increase the probability of the situation being resolved safely (Stranks, 1991).

In the event of a natural disaster, community medical and disaster resources might not be available. It is essential that school boards make disaster preparedness a priority and then leave the basic elements of a plan and list disaster and first-aid supplies for schools and first-aid supplies for classrooms (Portis, Mary and Portis, Richard, 1992).

While Arya (1995) stressed the need to educate the population through the use of mass media, and the children in their primary and secondary schools regarding do's and don'ts during and after earthquakes, the study of Faupel, et. al. (1992) indicated that participation in some type of disaster education programme is strongly related to the preparedness measures.

Sapire and Panaccione (1992) have reported that proper preparedness can reduce indirect consequences of earthquake such as mortality and morbidity.

Insights and tools are identified that may improve disaster preparedness, management, recovery, and learning (Smithson, 1990).

Earthquake Preparedness 101 (1992) gives the details of the studies at earthquake preparedness, examining particularly how to assess hazards, reduce hazards, educate the campus community, and acquire emergency equipment and supplies.

Regarding disaster preparedness, only a small percentage of all districts in earthquake-prone areas have earthquake and fire action plans (Heller, et. al., 1991).

Saunders (1992) reviews problems related to disaster preparedness.

Recommendations for Emergency Management Planning for School Facilities (1993) provides suggestions for developing an emergency preparedness education programmes are offered with crisis-intervention strategies for handling children's and personnel emotional responses to disaster.

According to Marks (1990) the preparedness programmes should be interesting, active, involve rehearsal, both imaged and actual, use group psychology and support, counteract psychological defences, and whenever possible make the procedures enjoyable, and even fun!

Disaster prevention, mitigation and preparedness are better than disaster response in achieving the goals and objectives of the Decade. Disaster response alone is not sufficient, as it yields only temporary results at a very high cost. Prevention contributes to lasting improvement in safety and is essential to integrated disaster management. The Yokohama Strategy and Plan of Action for a Safer World (1994) recommends that

(a) Disaster prevention and preparedness are of primary importance in reducing the need for disaster relief.

(*b*) Early warnings of impending disasters and their effective dissemination using telecommunications, including broadcast services, are key factors to successful disaster prevention and preparedness.

(*c*) Vulnerability can be reduced by the application of proper design and patterns of development focussed on target groups, by appropriate education and training of the whole community.

The most important need is to educate all citizens who will be ultimately responsible for implementing the pre- and post- disaster plans (Ganguly, 1993). Such education must begin at the early stage of schooling because it

(*a*) provides education which is contemporary and relevant,

(*b*) prepares for participation,

(*c*) combines past experience with recent trend,

(*d*) helps to develop affective domain abilities for collective work,

(*e*) promotes informed decision-making abilities.

Training and Skills

The importance, various behaviours and skills – of training in disaster preparedness are discussed in this section.

The Joint Assistance Center (JAC) at Gurgaon was set up after the devastating Andhra Pradesh cyclone in 1977, specifically for disaster preparedness (Disaster Management, 1982). The Center has regular programmes, which train people to deal with various kinds of disasters. The JAC work includes:

(*a*) Elementary level training course: Training in areas like first-aid, evacuation and rescue of victims – from the buildings, the hill-tops or isolated places, camping, tent pitching, use of indigenous techniques, ropes and knots, etc.

(b) Advance level training: Swimming, climbing, rowing, camp planning, surveys, contingency plans, co-ordination exercises, rock climbing, river crossing under different conditions.

(c) Motivational work: One day discussion groups, exhibitions to promote local techniques applicable in emergencies and one week leadership training programmes.

The National Workshop on "Role of Education and Training in Natural Disaster Management" (1998) recommended that

(a) Natural Disaster Management should be introduced as an activity based programme and not as a scholastic one.

(b) Modules generated in disaster management may be used in the pre-service and in-service training programmes of the District Institutes of Education and Training.

(c) At the college level it can be incorporated in the course content of the diploma Course in Environment Education.

Medina (1992) suggested

1. an outline of training module and training syllabus/ manual on disaster preparedness and management.

2. that training is vital in preparing the people in coping with natural disasters. It should be complemented by informational, motivational programmes for out-of-school youth and educational programmes for students at all school levels.

Goutam P.R. (1992) identified the goal of training related to disaster management is to minimise or eliminate loss of life and property arising out of disaster by maximising physical, material and intellectual resources. He also elaborated on the three domains of training—knowledge, skill and awareness/ motivation in the context of disaster.

According to Natural Disaster Reduction—South Asian Regional Report (1994), facilities for education and training in disaster reduction and management are not adequately developed in the region. The extent of mobilisation of human resources would be considerably enhanced if put in place. This would require technical training, skill development and attitudinal changes.

Organisation of American States (Organisation of American States, 1984) has taken up the Natural Hazard Pilot Project whose primer document's objective is to provide guidance on natural hazard management, including the selection of assessment and mitigation measures for specific hazards. The emphasis is on prevention by considering natural hazards issues early in the development process.

According to Raphel (1983):

(a) Training in the four elements of work included – how helpful the training had been in 'explaining the nature of disasters, in preparing emotionally for the work, in informing the potential pitfalls, and in providing new skills'.

(b) Empathy and identification are likely to be the key aspects of the type of work undertaken in the aftermath of disasters.

(c) A variety of skills and qualities of social workers were mentioned by users in the aftermath of the disasters. Those most frequently referred to were friendliness, honesty, and being supportive, patient, reliable, flexible, and able to listen. Friendliness, honesty and supportiveness related to the extent to which disaster workers frequently worked outside the 'normal' professional-client relationships, patience to the

extended period of time the work often taken, reliability to the extended period of time that the service needed to be in place, and flexibility to the non-directive role often perceived by users as being of greatest value.

According to Natural Disaster Reduction – South Asian Regional Report (1994), text-books at school levels may incorporate information about the disaster causing phenomena and the precautionary steps to be taken to reduce their impact in order to generate awareness among children.

Lunn (1990) described a course designed to provide the necessary skills and knowledge for emergency management.

Wenger (1978) argues that during disaster induced crisis states the traditional institutional structure is no longer collectively defined as an appropriate guide for behaviour, and that altruistic behaviour which is beneficial to the whole community is sanctioned more strongly than the traditionally dominant selfish activity, such as production, distribution and consumption of goods. At such times, the activity of the whole community is geared towards helping those who are suffering (Siporin, 1976) and a mandate is available for all public agencies to concentrate their resources on the task of disaster recovery.

Davies and Muir (1984) have commented that:

(a) Professional social workers in the mental health field often ignore the potential their clients have for helping others as well as themselves.

(b) The realistic planning requirements, are for post-impact provision of a broad range of human and social services which should be delivered by networks of established organisations and new groups, using professionals, para-professionals, and trained volunteer personnel knowledgeable about the community and its

resources, facilities and skills, and the dynamics of disaster. (Baisden and Quarantelli, 1981).

(c) If at the time of a disaster, there is an 'action' of grief, shock and fear, there is also a 'reaction' of sympathy, good-will, altruism and generosity. It is within this context that the role of social workers in responding disaster should be identified.

Carter (1992) concluded that a possible combination of desirable objectives for leadership in disaster management includes personal qualities, professional competence, self-confidence, sound judgement, accurate decision-making, ability to communicate, personal example and appropriate style.

Handmer and Penning-Rowsell (1990) summarise that:

(a) At the critical period 'Teachable Moment' people have specific problems, which may be of an emotional rather than practical nature, and are seeking information to help solve them. The problem-solving need should also be kept in mind when devising content, as people are unlikely to be seeking information for its own sake.

According to Brown J. (1990), the initiatives of publishing information leaflets, mounting exhibitions and providing a special service for schools call for a more informed citizenry who can contribute to national prosperity make better personal decisions and play a role in planning decisions.

In terms of changing behaviour many public education programmes appear to have been complete failures (Illinois Department of Transportation, 1980). Even if the criterion is simply to improve knowledge, there are few definite successes. It is stressed that the ability to impart knowledge is not by itself an ability to change behaviour: linkages between knowledge, awareness and behaviour are at present poorly understood.

According to Emergency/Disaster Planning for Principals 1992) the disaster plan should include among others the training requirement for staff and students. For the plan to be effective, it needs to be widely disseminated. Everyone who has some involvement in its implementation should be well versed in its contents. This can be achieved by providing regular exercises in which the procedures and arrangements to be used during an emergency are tested. This should consist of more than an evacuation to the school compound. The plan should describe a programme of exercises.

Training programmes have two essential tasks:

(a) identification of principles of action at a strategic level and

(b) teaching implementation techniques in a series of practical steps (Disaster Mitigation in Asia and the Pacific, 1991).

Disaster Management in India

In this part of the review, the responsibility, organisational machinery, institutions and focus – disaster preparedness in India are highlighted.

Natural Disaster Reduction—South Asian Regional Report, 1994 provides the following details with respect to disaster management in India:

(a) The primary responsibility for management of natural disasters in India vests with the State Governments. The National Government supplements the efforts of the State Governments in dealing with disaster situations and also provides the major part of financial resources for disaster response. There is an institutional arrangement at the National, State, District and Sub-district levels to deal with emergency situations. A National Contingency Action Plan exists for ensuring emergency assistance in the wake of

natural disasters at the National, State and District levels. The State Governments have their Relief Manuals/Codes which lay down the procedures and powers for emergency management and provision of relief.

(*b*) The National Organisational arrangements consist of a cabinet committee on Natural Disaster Management at the National Level, and a crisis management group presided over by the Cabinet Secretary. Disaster Relief Coordination is effected by a Central Relief Commissioner in the Ministry of Agriculture. Each State Government has a Relief Commissioner and State Cabinet Level Co-ordination Committees. At the District Level, District Collector presides over the Relief Committee which consists people's representatives.

(*c*) A Calamity Relief Fund (CRF) is allocated to each State on an annual basis, 75% of which is contributed by the Central Government. The quantum of the CRF is determined by independent Finance Commissions once in five years.

(*d*) The focus today is on disaster preparedness but with well-planned components of both mitigation and relief programmes. This approach demands strengthening of existing mechanisms and creating new ones for technology transfer, dissemination of technical know-how, and training thereby helping local institutions, community groups, NGOs and government agencies to cope with the related problems of preparedness and mitigation.

(*e*) Considering the severity of situation, the United Nations has declared the present decade as the International Decade for Natural Disaster Reduction (IDNDR). One of the cherished goals of the IDNDR is to develop the capacity of disaster prone countries to be able not only to cope with this challenge but also to reduce the disastrous effects by pro-active prevention and preparedness measures.

(f) In India, the health sector's disaster preparedness has been institutionalised with the objective to incorporate disaster plan in the health delivery system.

Where disasters are predictable, advance preparation holds the key to control and channelisation of human behaviour. During the October, 1989 San Francisco earthquake, the city's 'extraordinary performance' proved that 'for those who choose to live on the edge, it pays to be prepared.' In India, particularly in the disaster-prone north eastern region, this has been recognised as a major mitigating input and a recent high-powered committee made a detailed recommendation for preparedness in a co-ordinated manner (Das, H.N., 1994).

From the above review of related literature, it is possible to conclude that hunches for the objectives framed on page no.20 could be listed. Basing over this, the following hypotheses are formulated for continuing the study in the proper direction.

Hypotheses

The investigator proceeded with the following hypotheses to achieve the objectives of the present study:

1. There are certain natural disasters which recur regularly in India.

2. Certain behavioural traits are essential to meet disaster situations.

3. The essential behavioural traits to meet disaster situations can be developed through classroom activities at the primary school level.

4. The classroom activities to develop essential behavioural traits to meet disasters can be fused into the existing primary school curriculum.

Limitations

With respect to the sample, its variables, geographic area of investigation, and the years of study, certain limitations have been exercised due to the time factor. These limitations of the present study are given as follows:

(a) Sex of the sample is not taken into cognition.

(b) Socioe-conomic status of the sample is not considered in the study.

(c) The activities are applicable to Primary classes of I, II and III.

The research design, area covered by the investigator, selection of sample, development of the questionnaire and its administration is discussed in the third chapter.

3

RESEARCH DESIGN

The research design, area covered by the investigator, sample selected for the study, development of the questionnaire, pilot study, finalisation of the questionnaire, and administration of the questionnaire is discussed in the present chapter.

Research Design

In order to achieve the objectives, the present investigator proceeded in the following manner which is given as steps of the Research Design. They are:

1. Listing of the behavioural traits essential to meet disaster situations by combining opinions of the experts and literature survey.
2. Establishment of the behavioural traits essential to meet disaster situations in the light of opinion of the experts.
3. Preparation of activities to inculcate the behavioural traits essential to meet disaster situations.
4. Analysis of the curriculum of classes I, II and III for finding out the existence of activities that inculcate behaviours essential to meet disaster situations.

Area Covered by the Investigator

The geographical area covered by the study is India.

Tools Developed and Used

For achieving the first objective – 'to list out the disasters that occur in India with a natural trigger' – a review of journals and books was carried out. The details are discussed under section 3.7 in the present chapter.

A comprehensive list of behavioural traits of individuals to face natural disasters was developed through discussions with experts in the field of disaster management, research scholars and people in the disaster-prone areas. Basing over this, and review of related literature i.e., journals, Sociological Abstracts, Dissertation Abstracts, International correspondence with experts from India and abroad, Symposia literature, text-books and handbooks, a questionnaire was constructed for the purpose of realising the second objective i.e., 'to establish behavioural traits essential to meet natural disasters'. The details are discussed below:

Development of the Questionnaire

A questionnaire describing the behaviours essential to meet the disaster situations is developed in the following manner:

The concept of "Self" is taken into consideration while listing the behavioural traits essential to meet disaster situations. "Self" is described in terms of the mental processes that characterise the person and in terms of the meanings for the individual that result from these on-going processes (Prescott, 1957). The individual with favourable self-concept is a contributing member of the society which in turn will enable him/her to face the emergency situations. Further, the reactions of the individuals during the disasters depend on their emotions. So, the various emotions which have a bearing either directly or indirectly were taken up. For example, anxiety is shown as "sharing" behaviour while curiosity is expressed as "alertness". Affection indicates warmth, friendliness, sympathy or helpfulness.

Affection is indicated as sympathy by the one year old child which will continue as sharing things or ideas as he makes entry into school. The process of assimilating experience (i.e., gaining meaning) is speeded up tremendously when the child communicates with other persons. The child's meanings are common or shared; a word means the same to him as it does to all those with whom he comes into contact. These meanings are considered to be consensually validated in accordance with reality and logic as they are generally observed.

Parents give thought to helping children develop personality traits that will lead to good social adjustments. They try to teach children to co-operate, to be good at sports and to be unselfish (i.e., altruistic). Good personal and social adjustments developed by the end of second year lead to the development of favourable self-concept. This will in turn make the child take initiative which is expressed as a leadership quality (Hurlock, 1994).

By the time the child is 4-5 years of age the personality pattern gets established. A few important personality traits that set during this period are courage, enthusiasm, co-operation, altruism and sympathy (Hurlock, 1994).

The child who does not need an immediate solution to all his problems and free to take a problem solving approach instead, is spontaneous, creative and original. If his social experiences and relationships demean or isolate him, they produce strong emotions (such as enthusiasm) working for more satisfying roles and relationships. On the contrary, emotional identification (such as sympathy) permits more complex interpretations of the significance of the self and its roles in relation to objects, events and persons.

The child who assesses himself more honestly and accurately tends to be more realistic regarding his level of aspiration. If he wins roles that carry prestige and plays them successfully, these experiences enhance his confidence in himself and his eagerness to undertake more difficult roles (sportsmanship).

The individual personalises his/her reactions only when he/she makes decisions (or has decision-making ability) permitted by his/her self. He has an empathetic capacity of his own which enables him to sense when they are really valued.

The individual while interacting with the physical world distinguishes interactions among external objects and processes and eventually concepts of cause and effect and of orderliness in the universe (co-ordination). An individual with favourable self-concept will be able to solve problems on his own without relying on others (independent thinking). He is free of some of the forces which bear upon the child who feels inadequate.

Children are the most vulnerable section of the community. If they are unable to understand and rationalise the event, they may suffer from phobias, sleep disturbances, loss of interest in school work, and aggressive or undisciplined behaviour (the category most at risk is 8-12 years old). This is because the psychological processes involved in developing as a self include among others, reasoning. A happy child takes more initiative in play and takes on more leadership roles and makes a favourable impression on others (Bevli, et. al., 1981).

The self-mediated, self-oriented processes continue to set new goals for experience, learning, role-playing and inventing or creating and direct the behaviour of the individual towards their realisation. He becomes dynamic and he initiates events to accomplish goals which he himself has set and lead others. Thus, when the child interacts with others, he may find himself organising and directing the group.

Based on the above discussion, a comprehensive list of behavioural traits of individuals to face natural disasters is prepared. The meanings of the behaviours given by Hornby

(1996) are adopted for the study. They are explained briefly in the following paragraphs:

1. Adjustment: The trait 'adjustment' in the present study is viewed as – setting the things right; putting the things in order; regulating the things; and making the things suitable or convenient for use.

2. Affection and Friendliness: The behavioural trait affection and friendliness is viewed as possessing the individuals kindly feelings and showing or expressing kindness.

3. Alertness: Alertness is viewed in the following manner in the disaster situations. An alert individual is watchful; vigilant; nimble; and on the look-out against danger or attack.

4. Altruism: The unselfishness; and the principle of considering the well-being and happiness of others first, have been viewed as the behavioural trait of 'altruism'.

5. Co-operation: The trait 'co-operation' in the present study is considered as working together for a common purpose in the emergency situations.

6. Co-ordination: 'Co-ordination' is the ability to bring or put into proper relation and cause to function together or in proper order.

7. Courage: Courage is viewed in the present context as boldness; nerve oneself to a venture; courage to act upto what one believes or to be brave enough to do what one feels to be right; and the quality that enables a person to control fear in the face of danger or misfortune.

8. Decision-making ability: This is considered as the ability to decide and act accordingly; and judging the various aspects during a disaster.

9. Empathy: The aspect of sharing another person's feelings during the disaster situations is taken as 'empathy'.

10. Enthusiasm: The strong feeling of admiration or interest is viewed as constituting 'enthusiasm'.

11. Helpfulness: 'Helpfulness' is defined as the willingness to – do part of the work of another person; making it easier for somebody to do something or for something to happen; and doing something for the benefit of somebody in need.

12. Independent Thinking. Independent thinking is viewed in the present investigation as – acting or thinking upon one's own lines; unwilling to be under obligation to others; not relying on others; and not depending on authority or control.

13. Initiative: The aspects covering 'the capacity to see what needs to be done and enterprise enough to do it; without being prompted by others; and be the first to take action' – are considered as constituting 'initiative'.

14. Leadership: This trait constitutes – action of guiding or giving an example; give a person lead; encourage him by doing thing; and is in the lead.

15. Rationality: 'Rationality' is viewed as 'ability to reason'.

16. Realism: The aspects of – practical; and not moved by sentiment constitutes 'realism'.

17. Sharing: 'Sharing' is viewed as – giving away part of; and enduring jointly with others during the disaster situations.

18. Spontaneity: 'Spontaneity' constitutes the aspects of – a happening from natural impulse; and not caused or suggested by something or somebody outside.

19. Sportsmanship: "The willingness to take risks and is not down-heartened, if lost" aspect constitutes sportsmanship.

20. Sympathy: 'Sympathy' includes the aspects of – capacity of being simultaneously affected with the same feeling as another; tendency to share another person's or thing's emotion or sensation or condition; and mental participation with another in his trouble or with another's trouble during the disaster situations.

A questionnaire to assess and establish the essential behavioural traits to meet disaster situations is developed in the following manner:

Pooling of Items on a Questionnaire

The investigator constructed five items for each of the behavioural traits which are essential to meet the disasters. A pool of items containing 100 items was thus, prepared from various sources like journals, reference books and text-books, and with the help of experts in the field of disaster management and fellow research scholars. The items were constructed bearing in mind the disaster situations in general, pre-disaster situations, aspects during the disaster situations, aftermath of disaster situations, post-disaster situations covering the extensive relief, rehabilitation and reconstruction phases.

The items are in the form of – a portion of a question which will make a complete sense with any of the three given alternatives – a, b, or c. Among the three alternative reactions one complies with the behavioural trait for which it is written and is considered as positive reaction, that is, the individual with this kind of behavioural trait will be able to tackle the disaster situation in a better manner. The other two alternative reactions are (1) neutral – neither contributes nor apprehends the concerned trait, and (2) negative – gives an exactly opposite view of the trait. These aspects are described below with an example:

You are a witness of a natural disaster. After sometime, certain signs that indicate the recurrence of disaster appear. Then, will you:

(a) inform everyone of your place to vacate and move away?

(b) start planning for measures to protect yourself and others?

(c) act as per the directions of the majority?

This item is developed for assessing 'courage' at serial no. 31. In this example, the positive reaction is 'b'. start planning for measures to protect yourself and others?; the neutral response is 'c'. act as per the directions of the majority? While the negative reaction is 'a'. inform everyone of your place to vacate and move away?

The thus developed questionnaire consists of 100 items related to essential behaviours to meet the disaster situations (Appendix-A).

Description of the Questionnaire

The questionnaire consists of twenty behavioural traits necessary to face the disaster situations. For each of the behavioural trait synonyms have been worked out and basing on these synonyms, a questionnaire has been developed. The description of the questionnaire is given in the following paragraphs:

Adjustment

The investigator developed items 1, 2, 3, 4, & 5 to establish the behavioural trait 'adjustment'. Items prepared for this behaviour assess the individual's ability to set right; put in order; regulate; and make suitable or convenient for use the things in meeting a disaster situation. The items are given below:

1. A lot of corpses remains on the habitations. Then, will you

(*a*) leave that place and live elsewhere?

(*b*) wait for the others to clean up the locality?

(*c*) remove and perform the last rites and continue living there?

2. Clean utensils for cooking are not available. Then, will you

(*a*) struggle and clean the utensils?

(*b*) eat whatever is available?

(*c*) stop cooking and eating?

3. The buildings, trees, etc., get scattered on the road obstructing the movement. Then, will you

(*a*) move them aside so that the path is cleared of any obstruction?

(*b*) push the dismantled structures slightly so that you can move forward?

(*c*) take a longer route without touching the dismantled structures?

4. Many lives are lost and property is damaged. In such instances, will you

(*a*) assess the magnitude of damage and draw a plan to provide succour to the affected people?

(*b*) wait for the government to help in this regard?

(*c*) throw away the damaged property?

5. Houses collapse then, will you

(*a*) leave the place and live at some other area?

(*b*) set right the structures including the others' too?

(*c*) continue to live in whatever condition the house may be?

Items 1 and 2 find out the individual's ability to make suitable or convenient for use – the place after a disaster situation and the things during a disaster situation. Item no.1 finds whether the individual is willing to remove and perform the last rites for the corpses in the aftermath of a disaster. The item no. 2 reveals whether the individual struggles and cleans the utensils for cooking in such a situation.

Item no.5 tests the individual's ability to set right the things after a disaster by way of setting right the structures of the collapsed houses. Item no.4 assesses the ability to regulate the conditions after a disaster by way of drawing a plan to provide succour to the affected people. Item no.3 has been included to know the individual's ability to put the things in order, that is, the manner in which he clears the obstructions after a disaster has occurred.

Affection and Friendliness

The items 6, 7, 8, 9, & 10 constitute probing the individual's ability of – showing or expressing kindness and a helpful attitude; and kindly feeling in a disaster situation. The items are shown as follows:

6. Alongwith buildings many of the sign posts also get destroyed.

A stranger happens to ask you the location of a particular place while you are busy working. Then will you

(a) turn a deaf ear to his request because you are busy?

(b) take him to the requested place personally because the way is confusing?

(c) ask him to seek guidance from somebody else because you are busy?

7. Your neighbour is disheartened of losing a pet. Then, will you

(*a*) comfort him by doing your best while attending to your own work?

(*b*) ignore him because you have to attend to your own work?

(*c*) keep calm because no one can do anything?

8. Many people were injured and you have to leave that place. In such instances, will you

   (*a*) lift your injured neighbour and take him alongwith you?

   (*b*) postpone leaving the place until your injured neighbour becomes alright?

   (*c*) leave the place keeping your neighbour alone because many such cases are around?

9. Necessity develops for clean potable water. In such instances, when somebody asks for a glass of drinking water, will you

   (*a*) give him water as much as he drinks?

   (*b*) keep calm without replying?

   (*c*) politely refuse him?

10. There is inadequate supply of food material to the group. Then, if somebody asks for some extra food material, will you

    (*a*) blatantly turn down his request because food is scarce?

    (*b*) share the food from your quota?

    (*c*) convince him the inability to give extra food?

The items 6, 8 and 10 find out the necessity of showing or expressing kindness and a helpful attitude during and after a disaster situation. Item no. 6 is included to know the busy individual's inclination to personally guide a stranger when there are no indications of recognising the directions to proceed for a particular place in the aftermath of a disaster. The item no. 8 finds whether the individual lifts his injured neighbour and takes alongwith him, in the instance of evacuating a place due to the likelihood of a disaster. Item no. 10 reveals the individual's aspect of sharing the food from his quota with somebody who asks for an extra food packet when there is inadequate supply during a disaster situation.

Items 7 and 9 assess whether kindly feeling is essential in meeting a disaster situation. The item no. 7 finds whether the individual comforts the disheartened neighbour who lost his pet, while attending to his own work in the aftermath of a disaster. Item no. 9 is included to know the individual's giving somebody, drinking water as much as he drinks when he requests for it during a disaster.

Alertness

This behaviour is assessed by the items 11, 12, 13, 14 & 15 which find out whether —watchful; vigilant; nimble; and on the look-out against danger or attack —is essential for an individual to meet the disaster. These items are as follows:

11. During a heavy downpour from incessant rains, will you

    (a) keep calm and follow the track of amount of rainfall for assessing the possible oncoming of floods?

    (b) keep calm listening to the comments made by others?

    (c) keep calm because you are sure that government will take appropriate steps?

12. The property and lives are damaged. Hence, will you

(*a*) be watchful to protect yourself and your property to the maximum possible extent?

(*b*) just sit and pray because nothing could be done against nature?

(*c*) fall in line with others and do what they do?

13. You are requested to fetch a torch from neighbouring house. Then, will you

(*a*) return home quickly alongwith the torch, candle, etc. ?

(*b*) just go and return from the neighbour after asking him for the torch, candle, etc.?

(*c*) return home after long delay because you went searching slowly?

14. Burns occur to people, then, will you

(*a*) attend to the worst sufferer?

(*b*) attend all the sufferers in a manageable manner?

(*c*) concentrate on fetching and inviting a doctor to attend them?

15. You are living in a crisis-prone region, then, will you

(*a*) keep alert during nights by keeping yourself awake intermittently?

(*b*) carefully listen to what people discuss about the crisis?

(*c*) be happy as usual because nothing could be done ay an individual.

Item no. 11 assesses the individual's ability to be on look-out against danger or misfortune in the wake of heavy downpour by way of keeping track of the amount of rainfall for the possible oncoming of floods. Item no. 12 finds out whether individual has to be watchful to protect himself and his property at times of disaster.

Items 13 & 14 have been included to know whether being nimble is necessary in a disaster situation. Item no. 13 finds whether an individual returns home quickly alongwith some lightning source if he is requested to fetch from a neighbouring house in the event of a disaster. Item no. 14 reveals the aspect of attending all the sufferers in a manageable manner, if burns occur to people in a disaster. Item no. 15 finds the individual's being vigilant is of any help to him during a disaster by way of keeping alert during nights in a disaster-prone region.

Altruism

The unselfishness; and the principle of considering the well-being and happiness of others first during a disaster situation has been assessed by the items 16, 17, 18, 19 & 20. They are discussed below:

16. The Government authorities are taking up extensive relief work for victims of a disaster-struck area. Presuming you are in the situation, will you

    (a) involve yourself by cancelling all your other engagements?

    (b) join others after completing all your responsibilities?

    (c) depute somebody because you are busy with your prior engagements

17. You have to vacate the place with a short notice. Will you

    (a) pack your belongings and move out?

    (b) wait for further instructions from appropriate authorities?

    (c) help in packing the belongings of all the members around you with yourselves?

18. You have got information where food is being distributed. Then, will you

    (a) propagate this information and take as many people as possible with you to the spot?

    (b) request somebody to bring food for distribution?

    (c) plan for obtaining the maximum share of food for you and your family members?

19. During a drought period, a person asks for food grains. Then, will you

    (a) give as much as he needs because you have enough of them?

    (b) turn away his request because you have seen many such people?

    (c) ask him to go to the charity home?

20. Near your home, some unknown person got hurt and is bleeding badly. Then, will you

    (a) rush up and in order to stop bleeding from cuts use any clean cloth that is available immediately to you?

    (b) ask some other person to bring cotton and cloth to cover the wound?

    (c) immediately inform the authorities in order not to face any complications?

Items 16, 18 and 20, find out the necessity of the principle of considering the well-being and happiness of others first either by involvement, propagating the information, or attending to the injured during a disaster. The item no. 16 finds whether an individual involves himself by cancelling all his engagements if government authorities are taking up extensive relief work for the victims of a disaster-struck area. Item no.18 reveals the nature of individual to propagate information about food distribution and take as many people as possible to the spot in a disaster situation. Item no. 20 is included to know whether an individual uses any clean cloth to stop bleeding from cuts by rushing to an injured person, near his home in a disaster situation.

The 'unselfishness' aspect during a disaster has been assessed by items 17 and 19. Item no. 17 finds whether an individual helps in packing the belongings of all the members around him with his if he has to vacate the place at a short notice in the event of a disaster. Item no. 19 is included to know the aspect of giving as much as the person needs when he asks for foodgrains during a drought period.

Co-operation

Items 21, 22, 23, 24 and 25 have been included to find out the necessity of 'working together for a common purpose' during a disaster. These are given below:

21. A voluntary organisation has taken up the work of renovating old houses in your area which is frequently prone to disasters. Then, will you
    - *(a)* join the voluntary organisation and help them?
    - *(b)* suggest measures of renovation to the members of the voluntary organisation, if they listen to you?
    - *(c)* not interfere because none of the houses under renovation is yours?
22. In the aftermath of a disaster, you and a few others of your group have been assigned the work of distributing the relief materials. You suddenly fell ill. Then, will you
    - *(a)* go to bed for taking rest so that you can work better?
    - *(b)* continue to work alongwith others in distributing the relief materials without caring for your illness?

(*c*) try to work with them because they may think otherwise?

23. You are injured. Then, keeping the possible loss in view, will you

    (*a*) at others' insistence, stop working for sometime to attend to your injury?

    (*b*) make your friends attend to your injury first and then go for work?

    (*c*) continue the work without caring for the injury?

24. You are left out only with implements which are used for ploughing the land, and your friend has been left only with a piece of land. Then, will you

    (*a*) take your implements and work alongwith in your friend's field to satisfy both the families' needs?

    (*b*) lend your implements to him on a rental basis so that both the families are benefited?

    (*c*) keep your implements with you and try to acquire whatever land is available and work by yourself?

25. You are injured badly. A person is found lying in the debris and all the efforts of a relief-worker to remove him from there are going in vain. Then, will you

    (*a*) extend a helping hand to the relief-worker so that the person can be removed from the debris?

    (*b*) stand there and watch the relief-worker doing his duty since you yourself are in a bad condition?

    (*c*) ask other relief-workers to come and help him remove the person from the debris?

Item no. 21 assesses the individual's ability of joining the voluntary organisation and helping them in taking up the renovating work of old houses in an area frequently prone to disasters. Item no. 22 finds out whether the individual continues to work alongwith others in distributing the relief materials without caring for his illness in the aftermath of a disaster. Item no. 23 is included to know whether the individual continues to work without caring for his injury.

Item no. 24 assesses whether the individual takes his implements and works alongwith his friend in the friend's field to satisfy both the families' needs, in the event of a disaster where he is left with the implements and his friend with a piece of land. Item no. 25 finds out whether an injured individual extends a helping hand to the relief-worker so that the person lying in the debris is removed in the event of a disaster.

Co-ordination

The items 26, 27, 28, 29 and 30 under 'co-ordination' assess the ability to 'bring or put into proper relation; and cause to function together or in proper order'. The items are described below:

26. During floods, there develops a necessity for clean clothes, proper food and other relief material. At times a lot of such material supplied by Voluntary Organisations and people piles up at one place resulting in a waste. To overcome this problem, will you

    (a) take initiative and join hands with relief-workers for the distribution of material in a quick manner?

    (b) join hands only when asked?

    (c) allow the relief-workers to work on their own so that they may be held responsible for what they do?

27. In a crisis situation, while the relief work is going on, you feel that you are suffering from fever. Inspite of that, will you

(*a*) see that the work is completed by providing appropriate guidance to the workers concerned?

(*b*) lie on the bed and ask somebody to bring a doctor?

(*c*) stop working and go to the doctor for taking a check-up so that you can do better work next day?

28. In the aftermath of a disaster, during the reconstruction phase, will you

(*a*) concentrate on getting your house repaired first so that you can give shelter to others also?

(*b*) reconstruct your own while attending to the work of others?

(*c*) assess the damage and take up the reconstruction work fixing priority on the extent of damage that has happened?

29. In order to protect the common property of the locality, will you prefer to

(*a*) join other members alongwith your personal belongings in relief measures?

(*b*) join other members in relief measures only when others ask you?

(*c*) concentrate setting right your own things so that they may not disturb others?

30. Necessity arises to fetch water from well which is on the other side of the wall and hundreds of people are waiting on the opposite side. Then, will you

(*a*) give a long pipe after collecting charges so that the water can be drawn without any difficulty?

(*b*) ask them to collect water by going round the wall?

(*c*) break a portion of the wall and see that water is supplied quickly to all the people?

Items 26 and 29 assess the necessity of working together to face the disaster situation successfully. Item no. 26 finds whether an individual takes initiative and joins hands with relief workers in distributing the relief material quickly so that it is not piled up and wasted. Item no. 29 is included to know whether the individual joins other members with his personal material in order to protect the common property of the locality.

The remaining items, i.e., 27, 28 and 30 find out the aspect of bringing the things into proper relation so as to tackle the disaster appropriately. Item no. 27 reveals the aspect of individual's ability of completing the work by providing appropriate guidance to the relief-workers even though he is ill, during a disaster. Item no. 28 finds out the aspect of assessing the damage and taking up reconstruction work fixing priority on the extent of damage in the aftermath of a disaster. Item no. 30 finds whether the individual breaks a portion of the wall and see that water is supplied quickly to all the people, when necessity arises to fetch water from a well which is on the other side of the wall and hundreds of people are waiting on the opposite side.

Courage

Courage is assessed by posing items 31, 32, 33, 34 & 35, related to 'boldness; nerve oneself to a venture; to be brave enough to do what one feels to be right; and quality that enables a person to control fear in the face of danger or misfortune.

This is discussed as follows:

31. You are a witness of a natural disaster. After sometime, certain signs that indicate the recurrence of disaster appear. Then, will you

    (a) inform everyone of your place to vacate and move away?

(*b*) start planning for measures to protect yourself and others?

(*c*) act as per the directions of the majority?

32. Disasters and natural calamities are unavoidable. Do you think one should be prepared to

(*a*) face them boldly and try to survive as the axiom says fittest survives?

(*b*) take all possible preventive measures and if something still remains, then leave it to God?

(*c*) do only what the majority of people do?

33. In a series of disasters, that occurred at a particular place, you found a particular phenomenon of nature. Two days prior to the occurrence of a disaster, a noise was heard. Then, will you prefer to

(*a*) go to the spot top investigate alongwith your friends in order to know that mysterious phenomenon?

(*b*) report the matter to the Government so that they may investigate?

(*c*) give wide publicity through mass media so that someone may take up the investigation?

34. In a fire disaster, you saw an old man being caught in a fire. Then, will you

(*a*) specifically point out that old man and beg for protecting him with the fire officers?

(*b*) use wisdom and by wearing insulated material try to bring the old man out?

(*c*) inform members who are present at the site about an old man being caught in the fire?

35. In one of the worst floods, a child and many snakes are being swept away in flood waters. To save the child, will you

(*a*) use sticks and net because you are afraid of snakes?

(*b*) ask your friends to rescue him because you are afraid of snakes?

(*c*) seek the help of relief-workers to rescue him?

Item no. 31 finds out the individual's ability to nerve himself to a venture in terms of planning measures to protect himself and others, when signs indicate of recurrence of the same disaster appear. Item no. 32 is included to know the boldness aspect, by way of preparing the individual to face natural calamities.

Items 33 and 35 assess the quality that enables a person to control fear in disaster situations. Item no. 34 is included to know whether the individual alongwith his friends goes to the spot for investigation about the mysterious phenomenon which is likely to follow a disaster. Item no. 35 covers the aspect of an individual who is afraid of snakes, still saves a child who is carried away by flood waters alongwith snakes. Lastly, the individual's ability of using wisdom in saving the old man caught in a fire is assessed through item no.34.

Decision Making Ability

Decision making ability is included to find out the necessity of 'judging; and to decide and act accordingly during the disasters. Items 36, 37, 38, 39 and 40 are described as follows:

36. In a place, disasters are recurring. Then, will you prefer to

    (*a*) wait until the government measures are implemented?

    (*b*) form a small group of like-minded people and do something immediately?

(*c*) seek the opinion of elders for an act to be undertaken?

37. For the rehabilitation centre, the government has promised certain measures but did not implement the same. Will you prefer to

(*a*) take a decision about an alternative approach for rehabilitation and start working?

(*b*) remind the government as suggested by others?

(*c*) watch the situation because no one has asked you to do anything?

38. For meeting a crisis, a rehabilitation centre is being planned by the government. Based on your experience, will you

(*a*) leave the matter for the government to take a decision regarding the location?

(*b*) keep watching calmly because you do not have faith in things like rehabilitation centres?

(*c*) suggest an appropriate site for the best results?

39. Your opinion is sought for taking a certain implementable decision. Then, will you

(*a*) get upset about the things to be said?

(*b*) ask others to give their opinion first?

(*c*) express your views without any inhibitions?

40. You feel it is safe to come out into the open area. Then, will you

(*a*) see that all people around you also come out into the open area?

(*b*) make a proposal to come out into the open area and leave the choice to them?

(*c*) fall in line with what others are doing?

Item no. 36 finds whether an individual forms a small group of like-minded people to do something immediately if disaster recur in their place. Item no. 38 reveals the aspect of showing an appropriate site for a rehabilitation centre when the government plans for it to meet the disasters. Item no. 39 finds whether an individual expresses his views without inhibitions in the event of his idea being taken for an implementable decision during a disaster. The aspect of saving people around by an individual by asking them to come to an open area during a disaster is assessed through item no. 40.

The aspect of 'taking an alternative approach for rehabilitation which the government promised but has not implemented the same' is found through item no. 37.

Empathy

'Sharing another person's feelings'— an aspect of empathy is assessed by the items 41, 42, 43, 44 & 45. These items are shown as follows:

41. While watching a movie, a scene appears depicting a disaster in which a family is badly affected, will you

    (a) feel sad and express your emotion freely by narrating it to others?

    (b) take it easy because afterall it is a movie?

    (c) feel sad for a moment and recover immediately?

42. While going to office for work you have come across a family which is in a sad situation. Then, will you

    (a) stop and console them by cancelling your work?

    (b) grieve alongwith them and then go for work?

    (c) go for work first because work is worship and then come back to share the sadness of the family?

43. It is said that our elders have donated their entire property for the cause of national movement against

the British which was a national disaster. Do you think that their act is

(a) ridiculous because for a common man it makes no difference either to be under the Indian Government or the British Government?

(b) not meaningful because making the family to suffer at the cost of nation is not proper?

(c) probably right because one should do his best to mitigate the sufferings of the masses?

44. A family of three members approaches you and explains about the condition in which they are as a result of a disaster. Then, will you

(a) offer them shelter and see to protect them through rehabilitation?

(b) guide them to the Government Rehabilitation Centre by giving them appropriate directions?

(c) check from different angles about the truth of their story because many liars are enacting that way now-a-days?

45. Food packets are to be distributed by you. Then, will you

(a) do the job strictly as per the instructions given to you?

(b) give a few packets extra to the needy?

(c) forego your share and help others who really need the food?

Item no. 41 finds out whether the individual feels sad and expresses emotion freely when he watches a sad situation in a movie. Item no. 42 finds whether the individual by cancelling his work, stops and consoles a family in a sad situation which he comes across while going to office. Item no. 43 finds out that an individual is probably right when he has donated his entire property for the national cause during the freedom movement.

Item no. 44 assesses the individual's feeling of offering shelter and protecting through rehabilitation to the family which explains its plight as a result of a disaster. Item no. 45 is included to know whether an individual who distributes the food packets foregoes his share and helps others who really need the food.

Enthusiasm

Enthusiasm constituting the ability of the individual to show a strong feeling of admiration or interest is assessed by items 46, 47, 48, 49 & 50. These are given below:

46. A particular place is struck by disasters frequently. Then, will you

    (a) make a study to find out the reasons for the frequent occurrence of disasters, irrespective of the involved expenditure?

    (b) approach the government to undertake the study to find out the reasons for the frequent occurrence of disasters?

    (c) keep calm and pray to God because it is a natural phenomena?

47. Natural calamities can occur anywhere at anytime. Hence, do you think is it better to

    (a) organise camps regularly for making people ready to meet the situation?

    (b) enrol volunteers and provide them necessary training at the appropriate time?

    (c) do whatever the government or local authorities plan?

48. You are running a high temperature when you are working in a relief camp meant for victims of a disaster. Then, will you

   (a) take medicine and continue with the relief work?

   (b) take medicine and go for rest so as to continue the relief work later?

   (c) withdraw from relief work due to your ill-health?

49. In a rehabilitation centre suddenly the tools have become useless for want of repair. Then, will you

   (a) fix them up temporarily and continue the work?

   (b) ask the concerned authorities to repair or procure anew?

   (c) stop the work until they are repaired or new ones arrive?

50. In any crisis there are certain indications which foretell the oncoming disaster. For example, black clouds indicate the oncoming of cyclone. If you perceive such an indication, will you run to your residential area and

   (a) alert every member of the locality?

   (b) relax because the crisis may or may not happen?

   (c) watch the Government authorities doing their work?

Item no. 46 finds out whether an individual makes any study by himself to know the reasons for the frequent occurrence of disasters in his place. Item no. 47 assesses the necessity of organising camps regularly for making people ready to meet the disaster situations. Item 48 is included to know whether an individual continues to work in illness by taking medicine when he is working in a relief camp meant for the victims of a disaster.

Item no. 49 finds the ability of the individual to fix the tools temporarily and continue the work when they have become useless for want of repair in a rehabilitation centre. Item no. 50 finds out the ability of alerting every member of the locality on hearing the forecast of a disaster.

Helpfulness

Items 51, 52, 53, 54 and 55 under this behavioural trait assess the individual's —doing part of the work of another person; making it easier for somebody to do something or for something to happen; and doing something for the benefit of somebody in need. These items are given below:

51. Suppose you have a lot of resources and people are suffering due to disasters. Do you prefer to

    (a) set up a Trust which will look after the immediate necessities of the disaster-stricken area?

    (b) share your resources with people who approach you?

    (c) utilise resources for your family's benefit first and then others?

52. The Government has decided to erect shelters for the people who face natural disasters. Then, will you

    (a) volunteer to work without remuneration because it is for a sacred cause?

    (b) donate in a maximum possible manner either in cash or kind, if necessary?

    (c) give necessary information regarding the location, size, etc., of the shelters as and when asked by the officers concerned?

53. A lot of calamities are happening in your place. Then, will you

    (a) pray in church, mosque, temple, etc., alongwith others?

(*b*) visit the affected areas for helping people to recover and pray in church, mosque, temple, etc., alongwith others?

(*c*) try to improve yourself so that you can help others during the next time?

54. During a rehabilitation phase after a heavy work, you are tired and still have to visit ten more houses for finding out the facilities given to them. Then, will you

(*a*) stop moving for sometime and take rest to recover from fatigue?

(*b*) continue moving in the area though you are feeling drowsy for completing the day's work?

(*c*) attend only the important houses where the likelihood of the occurrence of some mistake is anticipated?

55. Your neighbour has lost everything. Then, will you

(*a*) share your belongings, if asked, with him during a part of a day?

(*b*) spend totally your time working alongwith him for his recovery with all your belongings?

(*c*) give him guidance, if asked, for obtaining the required financial assistance from the Government?

Doing something for the benefit of somebody in need is known through items 51, 53 and 54. Item no. 51 finds out whether a wealthy person sets up a Trust to look after the needs of the disaster-struck area. Item no. 53 reveals whether an individual helps the people of disasters area by visiting them and praying alongwith them for their recovery. Item no. 54 is included to know the individual's commitment for the victims of a disaster by way of looking after the facilities provided to them during the rehabilitation phase.

Item no. 52 finds out an individual's role in helping the Government by volunteering to work even without any remuneration to the cause of disaster victims. Item no. 55 reveals whether an individual helps his neighbours working alongwith them for their recovery during the disaster situations.

Independent Thinking

This behavioural trait covers the aspects of acting or thinking upon one's own lines; unwilling to be under the obligation to others; not relying on others; and not depending on authority or control. Items 56, 57, 58, 59 and 60 under this trait are shown below:

56. Do you think about disasters as to
    - *(a)* why do they happen?
    - *(b)* what others are probably thinking of them and obtain their views
    - *(c)* an ordinary natural phenomena?
57. During the relief operations in a disaster-struck area, will you ask the volunteers to
    - *(a)* take on the spot decisions?
    - *(b)* strictly follow the schedule given to them?
    - *(c)* contact and take suggestions from others?
58. During the search and rescue operations after the occurrence of a disaster, will you prefer to
    - *(a)* do the things as the situation demands?
    - *(b)* do as the suggestions given by others?
    - *(c)* seek the guidance of others and work?

59. Would you like to

    (a) give effective suggestions to the authorities regarding relief measures to be taken?

    (b) follow the suggestions given by the authorities and others with respect to relief measures to be taken?

    (c) discuss or argue regarding the relief measures to be taken?

60. For a person in crisis do you feel ti is good to

    (a) use one's own intellect?

    (b) listen to others who are away from the crisis situation?

    (c) listen to people who are away as well as those in the crisis situation and act accordingly?

Items 56 & 59 find out the importance of acting or thinking upon one's own lines by raising a question as to why disasters happen and by giving effective suggestions of relief measures in the aftermath of a disaster, respectively. Item no. 57 assesses the independence on authority or control by way of taking on the spot decisions during the relief operations in a disaster-struck area.

Item no. 58 is posed to know the unwillingness to be under the obligation to others by way of doing things as the situation demands during the search and rescue operations. The aspect of non-reliance on others by using one's own intellect in a disaster situation is assessed through item no. 60.

Initiative

Initiative covers 'the capacity to see what needs to be done and enterprise enough to do it; be the first to take action; and without being prompted by others. Items included in this category are 61, 62, 63, 64 & 65 as shown below:

61. In a function hall, you notice that there is a short-circuit and everybody is in a chaotic state. Then, will you

    (*a*) go and try to switch off the mains, though there is every chance that you may receive an electric shock?

    (*b*) contact the nearest electricity department to save the situation ?

    (*c*) stay alongwith others guarding the place to see that nobody goes near the live wires?

62. The news of a disaster has spread in the town, but not yet reached the remote places. Then, will you

    (*a*) try to inform the people of the remote places?

    (*b*) wait until others ask you to join in informing the people of the remote places?

    (*c*) leave it to others about informing the people of the remote places?

63. You have thought of evacuating to save yourself from the incoming disaster. You come across your neighbour who is not able to move quickly because of his heavy luggage. Then, will you

    (*a*) tell your friends to help by bringing him later?

    (*b*) go to him and extend a helping hand?

    (*c*) concentrate on your movement and later attend to him?

64. After a disaster, an extensive rehabilitation work has to be taken up and everybody is anxious of how to go about it. Then, will you

    (*a*) give ideas and struggle hard to see that they are materialised?

(*b*) give ideas and leave it to the local authorities to decide and give shape to your ideas?

(*c*) keep your ideas to yourself because they are precious and reveal them only when you are asked to?

65. Nobody takes any action to control the situation. Then, will you prefer to

(*a*) come forward to explore all the possibilities of safer places?

(*b*) discuss with others and explore the possibilities of safer places?

(*c*) keep quiet until somebody asks you to do so?

Items 61 and 64 find out 'the capacity to see what needs to be done and enterprise enough to do it'. Item no. 61 reveals whether an individual goes and tries to switch off the mains in the event of an electric short-circuit in a function hall when everybody is in a chaotic state. Item no. 64 finds whether an individual gives ideas and struggles hard to see that his ideas get materialised, when an extensive rehabilitation work is taken up.

Items 62 and 63 assess an individual's ability to act without being prompted by others. Item no. 62 finds whether an individual informs the people of the remote places about the news forecast. Item no. 65 reveals an individual's ability of extending a helping hand to a handicapped neighbour in evacuating the place, inspite of his heavy load. Item no. 65 finds out the aspect of 'being first to take action' by exploring all the possibilities of safer places when nobody takes any action during a disaster.

Leadership

Items 66, 67, 68, 69 and 70 under 'leadership' covers the aspects of —give person a lead; encourage him by doing thing; is in the lead; action of guiding or giving an example;

and direction given by going in front. The description is given below:

66. For the vulnerable group exposed to natural disaster, will you prefer to

    (a) take initiative for the permanent solution?

    (b) suggest to others to work for a permanent solution?

    (c) wait until an appropriate time arises?

67. A training programme to prepare people to meet the disasters is organised, will you

    (a) take up the responsibility voluntarily to assign duties and responsibilities to able people?

    (b) continue guiding others by following the instructions from the higher authorities?

    (c) follow the instructions of the authorities strictly and work alongwith them?

68. As a volunteer in relief camp, you are required to work for the cause of the victims of a disaster. Then, will you

    (a) motivate your friends to get ready for the task?

    (b) discuss for arriving at an opinion and then move to attend to the relief work?

    (c) do whatever other members are doing?

69. The Government authorities are not providing appropriate compensation to the victims of a disaster. Then will you

    (a) raise your voice for the sake of the people until the compensation is given?

    (b) suggest the victims of the disaster to pressurise the Government to give compensation?

(c) closely study the situation for an appropriate solution?

70. A crisis arises by overflowing of water from a reservoir due to heavy rains which is a regular phenomenon every year damaging the major crops. Then, will you

(a) form a group to see that the water is not wasted?

(b) suggest few measures to check wastage?

(c) join others who are already checking the wastage?

Item no. 66 finds out the importance of 'giving person a lead' by taking initiative for the permanent solution for the vulnerable group exposed to a disaster. Item no. 67 is included to know whether 'action of guiding or giving an example' in taking the responsibility voluntarily to assign duties to able people during a training programme to prepare them to meet the disasters.

The aspect of encouraging volunteers of a relief camp to get ready to face the victims of a disaster is known through item no. 68. Item no. 69 finds out whether the person is in the lead by way of raising the voice to provide compensation for the sake of victims of a disaster. Item no. 70 reveals the importance of 'direction given by going in front' by forming a group to see that water is not wasted during the overflowing of water from a reservoir at the times of heavy rains.

Rationality

This behavioural trait constitutes the aspect of 'the ability to reason' and is assessed by the items 71, 72, 73, 74 and 75. These items are shown below:

71. Intuitively you feel that there is an onset of some natural disaster because a similar situation which occurred earlier thoroughly was followed by a disaster. Hence, will you

(*a*) see that everybody vacates their houses in your neighbourhood and move to safer places by giving them the relevant information about the feelings that you have?

(*b*) perform poojas, tantric rituals, etc., and relax?

(*c*) just wait and observe whether your feelings come true again or not?

72. During post-disaster relief operation, you have received food packets enough for your family. Due to shortage of the supplies, the family living next to you in the camp has not received the supplies. Then, will you

(*a*) feel sorry for that family as you cannot offer them from your supplies since you yourself are not having sufficient food?

(*b*) offer to share with the other family whatever food supplies you have in anticipation that the next quota of food supplies received by the other family will be reciprocated?

(*c*) request other victims who have received the food supplies to come forward and share from each of their supplies to help this family because all are in the same condition?

73. Is it better to

(*a*) face the situation because of the necessity?

(*b*) take suggestions from others and do what others say?

(*c*) probe into the human errors that have aggravated the situation?

74. Stopping a natural disaster is humanly impossible. When such an incident occurs, will you

(*a*) check the past and apply the best possible solution?

(b) follow the solution applied by the majority?

(c) hold your fate responsible for facing such a disaster and wait for events to take their natural course?

75. You are separated from your family members and their whereabouts are not known to you. Then, will you

(a) inform the search and rescue team regarding your missing family members and attempt on your own to locate them in the meantime?

(b) wait for the mass media or the authorities concerned to display the information about missing people?

(c) leave their safety in the hands of God?

Item no. 71 covers the aspect of giving relevant information in the wake of intuition that disaster is likely to occur and see that everybody vacates the place. Item no.72 finds out whether an individual offers his share of meagre food supplies to a family which has not received the food packets in a relief camp. Item no. 74 reveals whether an individual checks the past and applies the best possible solution when stopping a natural disaster is impossible.

Item no. 73 gives an idea whether it is better to face the situation because nothing could be done during a disaster. Item no. 75 finds that when an individual is separated from a family during a disaster, he should inform the search and rescue team and also attempt on his own to locate them in the meantime.

Realism

'Realism' includes the aspects of practical; and not moved by sentiment which is assessed by items 76, 77, 78, 79 and 80 as shown below:

76. There has been a warning to evacuate from your place of residence due to the imminence of a disaster. Then, will you

    (a) stay back until almost all others move because you feel that the warnings are not always true?

    (b) shift alongwith the majority?

    (c) evacuate on the first warning call so that you may have enough time to shift to the safest area?

77. In order to prevent your area from possible disasters, a highly expensive plan is being prepared by the local authorities, then, will you

    (a) support their view because they have undertaken a useful task?

    (b) criticise it because funds can never be made available for such a huge task?

    (c) share the opinion of the majority and keep your own ideas with you?

78. While working in a relief camp you come across a person who is badly injured and certain to die. Then, will you

    (a) ask others to look after him and continue your relief operations to save the lives of other less injured persons?

    (b) stop at this person and continue attending to him upto his last breath?

    (c) move out and attend to all other injured persons by asking your assistants to look after him, whenever necessary?

79. You are living in a disaster-prone area and your ancestors also lived there. Then, will you

    (a) shift permanently your place of residence to an area which is unlikely to be hit by a disaster?

(b) change your place of residence temporarily, whenever you sense the likelihood of a disaster?

(c) make elaborate safety arrangements to protect yourself when a disaster occurs?

80. You have come across a badly mutilated person whose sight is unbearable. Then, will you

(a) inform the relief authorities to shift him to the hospital?

(b) bear the scene and try to provide first-aid including cleaning the victim?

(c) move away from the site because you cannot bear such a sight?

Items 76, 77 and 80 cover the 'practical' aspect whereas 'not moved by sentiment' aspect is assessed by the items 78 and 79. Item no. 76 finds whether an individual evacuates on the first warning call so that he may shift to the best safe place in the likelihood of a disaster. Item no.77 reveals whether an individual is able to judge the availability of funds for a highly expensive plan of preventing an area from a natural disaster. In a disaster situation whether an individual provides first-aid to a badly mutilated person even though the sight is unbearable, is found out by item no. 80.

Item no. 78 reveals whether an individual attends all other injured persons leaving his assistants to look after a person who is certain to die. Item no. 79 finds out whether an individual shifts permanently his residence to an area which is unlikely to be hit by a disaster.

Sharing

Sharing has two aspects – give away part of and endure jointly with others. The items which test these aspects are 81, 82, 83, 84 and 85. These are given below:

81. In a winter season, some natural calamity occurs like an earthquake or flood and every one has lost all his

belongings. The scarcity of blankets is very huge. Fortunately, you possess three blankets – one for you, one for your spouse and one for your little child. Two of your neighbours approach you and request for two blankets to be given because they are not having any blanket with them. Then, will you

(a) give two blankets to your neighbours and adjust yourself alongwith your spouse and little child in one blanket remaining?

(b) give one blanket to your neighbours and ask them to adjust within it because you need one blanket for you and one for your spouse and little child?

(c) provide the address of the place to your neighbours where the distribution of blankets is being made by the relief camp workers?

82. In a relief camp meant for the victims of a disaster, after distributing the gunny bags for receiving the foodgrains to be taken home, it is found that only one gunny is available but two persons – yourself and your friend – are left. Then, will you

(a) offer a part of supplies to your friend after your requirement is met?

(b) offer half of the supplies to your friend until the next batch of supplies is distributed?

(c) request your friend to wait until the next batch of supplies is distributed?

83. All your resources are dried up and with great difficulty you have prepared some food for yourself and other members of the family. A beggar who is hungry requests you to give some food. Then, will you

(a) give some food from yours because the beggar is also hungry like you?

(*b*) show him the place where free meals are served by the relief camp?

(*c*) politely ask him to go to the next door because you yourself do not have sufficient food?

84. During a heavy downpour which is likely to result in a disaster, one person is drenched totally because of the weak shelter. You are able to see him from your house which is better than his. Then, will you

(*a*) call him to come and stay with you in your house?

(*b*) oblige to provide shelter in case he requests?

(*c*) feel inconvenience if he comes and therefore, suggest some other shelter?

85. In your place of residence, there is a severe drought and only your well has enough water to satisfy the needs. Then, will you allow others to take water

(*a*) on humanitarian grounds, and according to their necessity?

(*b*) when they plead for water?

(*c*) in a strictly restricted manner to your friends and relatives?

Items 81, 82 and 83 assess the aspect of 'give away part of'. Item no. 81 finds out an individual's nature of sharing his things with others who are in dire necessity. Item no. 82 reveals whether an individual offers half of his supplies to his friend when they find that only one gunny bag is available to carry foodgrains during a relief camp. Item 83 indicates the aspect of giving some food to the hungry beggar inspite of an individual's possessing food sufficient for his requirement, after a disaster.

Items 84 and 85 cover the aspect of 'enduring jointly with others'. Item no. 84 finds whether an individual gives shelter to a person who is drenched because of his weak shelter during a heavy downpour. Item no. 85 reveals the aspect of the owner of the well allowing others to take water, on humanitarian grounds, from the lone well which has water during a drought.

Spontaneity

The aspects of 'spontaneity' are – happening from natural impulse; and not caused or suggested by something or somebody outside. The items 86, 87, 88, 89 & 90 assessing this trait is shown as follows:

86. A disaster situation demands every person to take immediate action. Then, will you

    (a) do what you feel right at that particular moment?

    (b) do the work only when you are given a work specifically?

    (c) observe others and immediately do whatever they are doing?

87. You come to know that water is leaking from a bund. Would you like to

    (a) try to close the small hole at once and shout for help?

    (b) shout and collect people both for repairing and protecting the bund?

    (c) go to the authorities and inform them to take appropriate action?

88. During a disaster you have not got your share of relief supplies, though there is a buffer stock of them. Then, will you immediately

    (a) shout at the distributors for their mischief and condemn them vehemently?

(*b*) become angry and write an application against the distributors to be given to the higher authorities?

(*c*) show your anger and sign on the application against the distributors prepared by others?

89. An individual is being carried away by flood waters. Then, immediately will you

(*a*) jump into the water to save him?

(*b*) confirm that the person is alive and then jump into the water?

(*c*) get freezed out of fear?

90. Due to heavy rains, a rail bridge is washed away. You see a train which is fast approaching. Then, will you immediately

(*a*) run against the train shouting to stop?

(*b*) search for some object which could be used to stop the train?

(*c*) think about the nearest station and go to report?

Items 86, 88 and 90 cover 'happening from natural impulse' whereas items 87 and 89 assess the aspect of 'not' caused or suggested by something or somebody outside'. Item no. 86 reveals the aspect of doing what the individual feels right at that particular moment in a disaster situation. Item no. 88 finds whether an individual shouts at the distributors for their mischief condemning vehemently when his share of relief supplies is not received inspite of having a buffer stock. Item no. 90 constitutes an individual's running against the train shouting to stop when a rail bridge is washed away due to heavy rains.

Item 87 covers the aspect of an individual's presence of mind by posing a question as to whether he closes the small hole of a tank bund immediately and shouting for help later when he knows that water is leaking from it. Item no.89 reveals an individual's nature to save a person by jumping into the water when he is carried away by flood waters.

Sportsmanship

Sportsmanship covers the aspect of 'willingness to take risks, and is not down-heartened if lost'. Items 91, 92, 93, 94 and 95 assessing this trait are given below:

91. You plan for a training programme to handle a disaster situation and do not get the expected participation from other members of the society. Then, will you

    (a) continue to motivate people to participate in the programme, inspite of their opposition?

    (b) change the programme due to lack of expected response?

    (c) respect the opinion of the majority and do what others say?

92. While working for a relief camp, by mistake you have not followed some prescribed norms. The authorities have scolded you badly. Then, will you

    (a) leave the work abruptly because your ego got hurt?

    (b) inform others and obtain some solace for continuing the work?

    (c) continue working without getting disturbed because the mistake was yours?

93. As a volunteer of a relief programme, you are teased by your own colleagues. Then, will you

    (a) still continue to be in the camp alongwith them?

    (b) try to avoid the trouble-makers?

(*c*) complain about their behaviour to the organisers and see that they are set right?

94. There is a selection of volunteers for relief work and you are not included in the team. Then, will you

(*a*) voice your opinion against the decision?

(*b*) accept the decision of the selection committee because you respect them?

(*c*) share the work with others even though you are not included in the team?

95. You lost everything alongwith many other members of your area. One such member happens to be your closest rival and is in a bad state. Then, will you

(*a*) try to help him to the maximum forgetting your past rivalry?

(*b*) inform his friends about the bad condition in which your rival is and ask them to help him?

(*c*) keep quiet as you yourself are suffering from a severe loss and not in a position to help anyone?

Item no. 91 reveals the aspect whether an individual motivates people to participate in a training programme to handle disaster situation inspite of their opposition. Item no.92 finds whether an individual continues to work without disturbance in a relief camp if the authorities scold him for his mistake of not following the prescribed norms. The volunteer continuing in the relief camp even when his colleagues tease him is found by item no. 93.

Item no. 94 finds whether an individual shares the work even though his name was not included in the selection of volunteers for relief work. Item no. 95 reveals whether individual helps his rival who is in a bad state as a result of disaster.

Sympathy

Sympathy is assessed by the aspects of – capacity for being simultaneously affected with the same feeling as another; tendency to share another person's or thing's emotion or sensation or condition; and mental participation with another in his trouble or with another's trouble. The items covering these aspects are 96, 97, 98, 99 & 100. These items are as follows:

96. A person who has experienced the suffering from disaster narrates his tale of woes. Then, will you

    (a) believe it and give something, immediately to enable him to recover?

    (b) enact a few gestures and spell-out certain sympathetic words?

    (c) turn him away by saying that you are busy because such things are very common?

97. You have come across a person who is injured and unable to move. You are already holding sufficient load. Yet, will you

    (a) lift that person and take him to a safer place?

    (b) ask him to wait until you keep the load at some place and return?

    (c) keep on moving because the load is bothering you?

98. During the relief operations, you come across one of your old enemies who harmed you a lot, and now he is in an extremely poor condition. Then, will you

    (a) go to him and try to share his sufferings to relieve his mental agony?

    (b) ignore him and mind your own business?

    (c) ask your friend to help him because you are not in talking terms with him?

99. During a relief programme, you see a person who is taking the extended help twice through cheating the authorities. You are aware of the fact that this person is having a very large family and is badly in need of the material. Then, will you

    (a) keep quiet as if nothing had happened?

    (b) share your belongings with that person in order to help him more?

    (c) ask him to return the excess because cheating is a sin?

100. A few of the cattle are caught in a serious situation. Then, will you

    (a) save them even if it is risky for you because the cattle also are living beings?

    (b) save them if it is not risky for you because you have to protect yourself also?

    (c) if it is risky, then, save them by informing others who are competent in such activities?

Items 96 and 100 cover the aspect of 'capacity for being simultaneously affected with the same feeling as another'. Items 97 and 99 assess the 'tendency to share another person's or thing's emotion or sensation or condition' while the aspect cf 'mental participation with another in his trouble or with another's trouble' is found by item no. 98.

The aspect of believing the suffering of a person as a result of disaster and giving something immediately for his recovery is assessed by item 96. Item no. 100 finds whether an individual saves cattle at times of risk when they are caught in a disaster. Item no. 97 reveals whether an individual who is having sufficient load lifts an injured and handicapped person during a disaster to reach a safe place. Item no. 99 is included to know whether an individual shares his belongings with a person who is having a large family and cheating the authorities by taking the relief supplies twice in order to help him more. The aspect of an 'individual's sharing the suffering for relieving mental agony of an old enemy who harmed him a lot' is assessed by item no. 98.

Distribution of Items on the Questionnaire

The five questions, thus, developed for each behavioural trait are arranged in an ascending order and its distribution is shown in the table 3.1.

As the sample proposed to be used for the present study is of two kinds, namely, (1) Experts in the field of disaster management and (2) Field personnel and students, the investigator felt the need of preparing the questionnaire in two forms. One of the forms meant for experts has the items in the manner of suggestions – or in third person – that is, a suggestive tone. Whereas, the other form prescribed for field personnel and students, the items posed are addressed directly – or in second person.

The Pilot Study

The questionnaires shown as, are used for the pilot study. The purpose of the pilot study is to find any difficulties associated with administration, understanding the nature the and content of the items, the feasibility of the questionnaire and the like.

The pilot study was conducted on five locally available experts in the field of disaster management and ten locally available field personnel and students.

The responses of the questionnaire during the pilot study indicated the following improvements to be made in it. They are:

1. Ten items among 100 are inappropriate, and hence, have to be removed.

Table 3.1: Distribution of Items on the Questionnaire

Sl. No.	*Behavioural trait*	*Serial number of item in the Questionnaire*	*Total number of items*
1.	Adjustment	1, 2, 3, 4 & 5	5
2.	Affection and Friendliness	6, 7, 8, 9 & 10	5
3.	Alertnesss	11, 12, 13, 14 & 15	5
4.	Altruism	16, 17, 18, 19 & 20	5
5.	Co-operation	21, 22, 23, 24 & 25	5
6.	Co-ordination	26, 27, 28, 29 & 30	5
7.	Courage	31, 32, 33, 34 & 35	5
8.	Decision-making Ability	36, 37, 38, 39 & 40	5
9.	Empathy	41, 42, 43, 44 & 45	5
10.	Enthusiasm	46, 47, 48, 49 & 50	5
11.	Helpfulness	51, 52, 53, 54 & 55	5
12.	Independent Thinking	56, 57, 58, 59 & 60	5
13.	Initiative	61, 62, 63, 64 & 65	5
14.	Leadership	66, 67, 68, 69 & 70	5
15.	Rationality	71, 72, 73, 74 & 75	5
16.	Realism	76, 77, 78, 79 & 80	5
17.	Sharing	81, 82, 83, 84 & 85	5
18.	Spontaneity	86, 87, 88, 89 & 90	5
19.	Sportsmanship	91, 92, 93, 94 & 95	5
20.	Sympathy	96, 97, 98, 99 & 100	5
		Total	100

2. A few items have to be reshuffled to avoid monotony and boredom.

3. The alternative reactions of some of the items have to be modified, rephrased, or replaced totally.

4. The grammatical errors of few items have to be corrected.

The items found inappropriate in the questionnaire are:

Item no. 43 was removed because of the cultural bias inherent in the item which comes under 'empathy'. Item no. 81 which assesses the behaviour 'sharing' was rejected as it is too lengthy, confusing and there is a remote chance of such occurrence.

Item no. 33 coming under 'courage' was found inappropriate because of its similarity with item no.71 under 'rationality' and item no.50 under 'enthusiasm'.

Item no. 63 of 'initiative' was removed as there were enough items of the kind of 'evacuation', 'heavy load', 'neighbour'. Item no. 27 of 'co-ordination' was found inappropriate because a similar item exists under 'enthusiasm' as item no. 48. Item no. 38 under 'decision-making ability' was removed as the item is not relevant, in the sense that the planning of a rehabilitation centre by the government for meeting a crisis is in the hands of the government and people and a similar case was reported in Latur prior to an earthquake in 1993.

Item no. 2 assessing 'adjustment' was found not appropriate because it involved the non-availability of clean utensils for cooking and a similar aspect is taken care by many items as 'food grains' or 'food packets' under items 10, 19 and 45. Item 9 under 'affection and friendliness' which finds 'whether an individual gives somebody a glass of water' was removed as items 83 and 45 are of similar nature. Item no. 23 under 'co-operation' was removed because, continuation of work inspite of injury or illness exist as items 22 and 25. Item no. 100 under 'sympathy' finding out if the individual saves cattle in the event of risk during a disaster is inherently inappropriate and hence, was removed from the questionnaire.

Thus, in all, ten items were removed from the questionnaire.

The items which were re-written/modified/rephrased based on the suggestions of the pilot study are as follows.

The two alternative reactions – b. and c. for item no. 97 under 'sympathy' were changed partially. The alternative reactions b. and c. for the item 62 under 'initiative' were re-written. The alternative reaction a. for item no. 77 is changed while the stem of item no. 71 has been re-written which come under 'realism'.

The stem of item no. 78 under 'realism' was modified. The alternative reaction b. of item no.1 under 'adjustment' was replaced by an appropriate reaction. Similarly, the alternative b. of item no. 3 was also replaced totally which falls under 'adjustment'. The alternative b. of item no. 12 under 'alertness' was modified appropriately.

The alternative reaction a. for item no. 29 falling under 'co-ordination' was re-written appropriately. For item 34 assessing 'courage', the alternative reaction c. was modified appropriately. The alternative c. for item no.39 under 'decision-making ability' was rephrased to suit the behavioural trait. The alternative reaction c. for item no. 60 under 'independent thinking' was modified appropriately.

The alternative c. for item no. 75 assessing 'rationality' was replaced totally with an appropriate alternative reaction. The stem of item no. 95 finding the 'sportsmanship' was modified to suit the purpose. The alternative b. of item no. 20 was lightly modified according to the behavioural trait at hand. All the three alternatives of item no. 85 were rephrased to suit the purpose.

The suggestions made as a result of the pilot study are incorporated in the questionnaire and the final tool consisted of reshuffled items which is total to 90.

The reshuffled items are shown in the table 3.2 on the next page.

Table 3.2: Reshuffled Items in the Final Questionnaire

Sl.No. in the original questionnaire	*Sl.No. in the final questionnaire*	*Sl.No. in the original questionnaire*	*Sl.No. in the final questionnaire*
1	54	26	42
2	x	27	x
3	50	28	31
4	81	29	57
5	73	30	85
6	47	31	15
7	51	32	1
8	77	33	x
9	x	34	69
10	88	35	75
11	25	36	9
12	72	37	13
13	90	38	x
14	76	39	68
15	80	40	89
16	30	41	10
17	56	42	16
18	74	43	x
19	86	44	48
20	64	45	67
21	24	46	2
22	39	47	3
23	x	48	33
24	65	49	37
25	70	50	66
51	20	76	26
52	14	77	22

Sl.No. in the original questionnaire	*Sl.No. in the final questionnaire*	*Sl.No. in the original questionnaire*	*Sl.No. in the final questionnaire*
53	11	78	43
54	44	79	60
55	49	80	71
56	6	81	x
57	45	82	38
58	41	83	52
59	53	84	61
60	55	85	78
61	12	86	5
62	21	87	17
63	x	88	32
64	28	89	62
65	58	90	79
66	8	91	19
67	4	92	40
68	34	93	36
69	46	94	63
70	83	95	84
71	23	96	7
72	27	97	18
73	59	98	29
74	82	99	35
75	87	100	x

(Where x means that item is removed)

The Final Questionnaire

The item numbers and the corresponding behavioural trait in the final questionnaire is given in the table 3.3.

Table 3.3: Distribution of Items on the Final Questionnaire

Sl.No.	*Behavioural trait*	*Serial number of item on the final Questionnaire*	*Total number of items*
1.	Adjustment	50, 54, 73 & 81	4
2.	Affection and Friendliness	47, 51, 77 & 88	4
3.	Alertness	25, 72, 76, 80 & 90	5
4.	Altruism	30, 56, 64, 74 & 86	5
5.	Co-operation	24, 39, 65, & 70	4
6.	Co-ordination	31, 42, 57 & 85	4
7.	Courage	1, 15, 69 & 75	4
8.	Decision-making Ability	9, 13, 68 & 89	4
9.	Empathy	10, 16, 48 & 67	4
10.	Enthusiasm	2, 3, 33, 37 & 66	5
11.	Helpfulness	11, 14, 20, 44 & 49	5
12.	Independent Thinking	6, 41, 45, 53 & 55	5
13.	Initiative	12, 21, 28 & 58	4
14.	Leadership	4, 8, 34, 46 & 83	5
15.	Rationality	23, 27, 59,82 & 87	5
16.	Realism	22, 26, 43, 60 & 71	5
17.	Sharing	38, 52, 61 & 78	4
18.	Spontaneity	5, 17, 32, 62 & 79	5
19.	Sportsmanship	19, 36, 40, 63 & 84	5
20.	Sympathy	7, 18, 29 & 35	4
		Total	90

The final questionnaire is in two forms – one, meant for experts and another for field personnel and students.

Selection of the Sample

The sample selected for the present investigation was the people concerned with the field of disaster management. The range of sample was from experts both in India and abroad, apart from the students in the fields of education and social work and the relief-workers from National and International bodies who had a direct bearing over the disaster victims. In all, 68 experts were listed from the available resources like Asian Disaster Preparedness Center, Bangkok; Indian Institute of Public Administration, New Delhi; National Institute of Rural Development, Hyderabad; Tata Institute of Social Sciences, Bombay. Similarly, 64 field personnel and 13 students were listed from resources like Directory of Voluntary Organisations, 1993; Books; Osmania university, Hyderabad.

Realisation of the objectives

As mentioned earlier on page no.41 for realising the first objective, a review of journals and books, discussion with research scholars, supervisors and experts in the field of disaster management is made to prepare a list of common and frequently occurring natural disasters in India.

The most common natural disasters in India are avalanches, cyclones, drought, earthquakes, famines, floods, and landslides. Volcanic eruptions are uncommon in India. In addition to the above, the concept of 'El Nino' is also given. The detailed description of the various natural disasters that occur in India alongwith its causative factors and its occurrence is given below:

Avalanches

Avalanches occur when snow on slopes suffers from structural weaknesses and these are often caused by changes within the snow pack. A large overburden of snow may remain unstable because it is anchored to a solid underlayer or occurs on a slope which is too shallow to enable it to move. On the other hand, a small layer may be unstable because it is not bonded well to snow or the ground underneath. Snow avalanche hazards are greatest on slopes in the range 25 to 40 degrees: lower angles do not encourage failure of the snowpack, while at higher angles there is less opportunity for the snow to build up to unstable thicknesses. For these reasons, snow avalanches are uncommon on slopes that are shallower than 15 degrees or steeper than 60 degrees (Alexander, 1993).

Avalanches constitute a major hazard in the higher reaches of Himalayas. Parts of Himalayas receive snowfall round the year and avalanche-spots are in abundance. Scene of severe snow avalanche actions can be observed during and after winter snowfalls in Jammu & Kashmir, Himachal Pradesh and the hills of west Uttar Pradesh (Rao, 1994).

Cyclones

Tropical cyclones are intense low pressure systems in the tropics. Air spirals at speeds exceeding 120 kilometres per hour around the centre of these lows, like a giant whirlwind (Hazards, Disasters and Survival, 1992).

Earth's atmosphere consists of a constantly changing patterns of high and low pressure cells, which are depicted on weather maps by roughly circular or elliptical isobaric configurations known as anti-cyclones (highs) and cyclones (lows). Such pressure systems generally cover tens of thousands of square kilometres and move at varying speeds across the earth's surface. For a high-pressure area to be maintained, air must descend vertically within it, thereby warming, tending to become dry and clear and flowing outwards at the surface (Figure 3.1a). Conversely for a low-pressure area to be maintained, air must rise within it, thus becoming cooled tending to form clouds and precipitation and drawing air inwards to the low-pressure centre (Figure 3.1b).

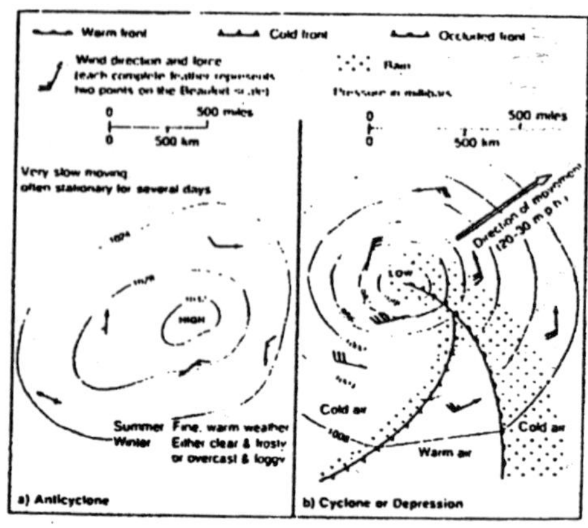

Figure 3.1: Weather features of high and low-pressure systems in the Northern Hemisphere (air movement in the Southern Hemisphere is in the opposite directions) (a) Anticyclone; (b) Cyclone or Depression.

In the Northern Hemisphere the earth's rotation causes the wind to be deflected to the right, resulting in a counterclockwise spiral around the low-pressure centre-whilst in the Southern Hemisphere the situation is reversed, causing a clockwise spiral. Such circular motions as these are termed votices, which vary in size from the smallest dust devils, through the tornadoes, upwards to the larger hurricanes and cyclones.

Andhra Pradesh has witnessed major cyclones frequently, for example, 1976, 1977, 1979, 1983.

The coastline of India affected by 5 to 6 cyclones every year out of which 2 or 3 may be severe. Cyclones occur in the months of April/May and October/November (Pasrija, 1991).

Drought

Drought is a lack of sufficient water to meet essential needs for an unusually long period. However, for statistical convenience the true climatic desert has been defined cartographically by the 100 millimetres (0.4 inches) annual precipitation line (termed an isohyet). Calculations have shown that within this zone there is a permanent water deficit, because potential evapo-transpiration is so high that it exceeds the total rainfall by a factor of at least ten (Whittow, 1980).

The dearth of rainfall in the arid zone may be caused by one or more factors. In the first place aridity may result from a location in a continental interior, far removed from the moisture-laden oceanic winds, as in the case of central Asia. Secondly, the region may lie in the 'rain shadow' of a major mountain range, and thirdly, we have the coastal deserts which exist because winds, having blown across a cool ocean current on to a heated land, do not condense their moisture into anything more than mist. The major tropical deserts which coincide with large, permanent high-pressure systems, in which air is slowly subsiding before blowing outwards at the surface (Whittow, 1980).

Drought-prone Area in India is 33 per cent which receives less than 750 mm rainfall annually. Another 35 per cent area falls under medium rainfall region (Jaiswal & Kolte, 1981).

In 1966, India experienced one of the worst droughts in the recent history, caused due to widespread failure of monsoon in many parts of the country. The worst-affected states during kharif season were Gujarat, Maharashtra, Karnataka, Rajasthan and Orissa. Kharif crops, particularly rice, were seriously affected in the parts of Uttar Pradesh, Bihar, West Bengal and Tamil Nadu. Rabi crops also failed due to scanty and untimely rains. Food production fell short by 16.7 million tons of the requirements. As a result, scarcity conditions developed in the State of Andhra Pradesh, Gujarat, Karnataka, Maharashtra, Madhya Pradesh, Orissa and Rajasthan. Out of a total 330 districts in the country, 125 were affected. In Maharashtra, scarcity conditions came to stay with more disastrous effects during 1966-67 (Jaiswal & Kolte, 1981).

On account of the failure of the south-west monsoon severe drought was experienced in Gujarat, Maharashtra,

Rajasthan, parts of Andhra Pradesh, Bihar, Haryana, Karnataka, Uttar Pradesh and West Bengal during 1972-73. Considering the magnitude and time factor of the scarcity conditions in Maharashtra on account of continuous crop failures for three years since 1970-71, the situation may well be described as 'famine' rather than a 'temporary scarcity' (Jaiswal & Kolte, 1981).

Earthquakes

Earthquakes result from rocks breaking under stress which build up beneath the earth's surface as a result of the constant movement of the jigsaw-like pieces that make up the thin outer shell of the earth (Hazard-wise: Emergency Management Australia, 1995) Earthquakes (Tatsch, 1977) may be caused due to one or many factors of the following:

1. earth's seismo-tectono-magmatic behaviour
2. the state of stress
3. variations in polar motion, and
4. impounding of water in reservoirs.

Active seismic zones constitute 56.3 per cent of total area amounting to 3.3 million square kilometres. The most susceptible area for earthquakes is northern region from Kashmir to Arunachal Pradesh. Peninsular region is more or less stable with some minor seismic activity.

The Andaman islands, Assam and major parts of Himalayas form part of Alpine belt which is highly earthquake-prone. The Himalayan ranges from Kashmir to Assam, Indo-gangetic plains, the Kutch and Kathiawara region of Western India are geographically the most vulnerable parts of the country (Disaster Management, 1984)

Earthquakes are becoming more frequent after the relative quiet of 1950-1980 (Michaelis, 1992).

Famine

Famine is an extreme scarcity of food often associated with extended drought conditions.

The causes of famine are broadly classified as 'natural' and 'artificial'. Natural causes include droughts, floods, earthquakes, unseasonable cold weather, plant disease, attack of locusts, etc., whereas the only important artificial cause is war. There are also socio-economic causes of famines, for example, in India 'there are more famines of work than of food'. Negligence on the part of State and people's poverty may also be contributory factors in recurrence of famines (Kulkarni, 1990).

The years of relatively widespread scarcities since independence are 1952-53, 1965-67 and 1970-73. In 1952-53 there were crop failures in some parts of the country. But the scarcity was temporary and followed by two years of bumper crops, 1953-54 & 1955-56.

Floods

Floods are defined as the overflowing of a river (State of India's Environment, 1991).

Flooding in coastal areas may be caused by the sea rising several meters above normal levels. Severe flooding, both near the coast and further inland, is caused by the combination of torrential rain and a simultaneous rise in sea level.

Flooding (Whittow, 1980) results from a variety of causes:

A. Fluctuations within the hydrological cycle

1. Rainstorm-river floods
2. Snowmelt floods
3. Coastal floods due to meterological conditions and seismic sea-wave.

B. Other causes

1. Dam or levee failure floods
2. Floods due to the rupture of a glacial lake
3. Floods resulting from landslides and volcanic events
4. Floods induced by land subsidence along coastlines.

Four flood regions (Disaster Management, 1984) according to river systems are:

(i) Brahmaputra region - Brahmaputra and Barack rivers and tributaries

(ii) Ganga region—Ganga and its tributaries

(iii) North-West region—Indus and its tributaries

(iv) Central India and Deccan region—Narmada, Tapti and East-flowing rivers.

Coastal areas of West Bengal and north Orissa, the areas north of Godavari to north of Nellore in Andhra region, the eastern south of Pondicherry, coastal areas along the Gulf of Kutch, parts of Tamilnadu and Orissa. Generally, regions that experience large floods occur where there is little vegetation, steep slopes, and many gullies, soils which are impervious to water and rocks which allow water to flow quickly to rivers.

Landslides

A landslide is caused by a geological instability of the slope because of heavy rain, earthquake, mining, construction, etc.

The forces that promote mass movement can be divided into external and internal categories. The exogenic causes of slope instability include steepening or heightening the profile, removing the lateral or underlying support, and loading the upper edge as a result of construction, land fill dumping (Alexander, 1993).

These factors are complemented by the endogenic or internal causes of landslides. Weathering involves disintegration that weakens soil and decreases its resistance to shearing. Deforestation or other kinds of devegetation can also weaken a slope, as the roots of plants tend to hold soils together, accounting for up to 90% of stability on certain slopes. The stabilising effect persists even for a certain period after the plants have died, until the roots decay. But the most important among endogenic causes is increased infiltration of water, which can lead to soil saturation. It may result from ploughing or from poorly organised drainage on a slope that has been modified by deforestation or urbanisation. Saturation increases pore water pressure which exerts a positive force that may cause the slope to fail (Alexander, 1993).

Landslides may also happen in flatlands where there are sharp differences or fractures between land levels, for example, in or near towns situated on high-river banks, landslides may cause a considerable damage.

Mountainous regions of Himachal Pradesh, Jammu & Kashmir and Uttar Pradesh are proned to severe avalanches while landslides have occurred even in states like Tamil Nadu and West Bengal where hilly areas like Ootacamund and Darjeeling are affected (Rao, 1994).

The incidence of landslides in Himalayas and other hill ranges in India is an annual and recurring phenomenon. Based on the experience of field studies carried out by Central Road Research Institute, New Delhi, the variation in degree of landslide incidence in various hill ranges can be grouped as shown in the table 3.4.

The most common volcano is a cone-shaped mountain built up by many eruptions and consisting of layers of lava and ash.

Table 3.4: Landslide Incidences in India (General Report on Landslides, 1989)

Hill Ranges	*Landslide incidence*
Himalayas	Very high to high
North-Eastern Hill ranges	High
Western Ghats & Nilgiris	High to moderate
Eastern Ghats	Low
Vindhyas	Low

Volcanic Eruptions

The volcanic disasters are uncommon to India. However, Andaman Archipelago islands lie in the seismo-tectonically active belt and form the converging plate boundary of India ocean. There are only two known active volcanoes in India—Narcondum and Barren islands, located in the Bay of Bengal about 130 kilometres north-east of Port Blair. The Barren island volcano remained dormant for nearly 200 years and erupted in March, 1991 and continued till November, 1991 (Tiruvengadachari, 1994).

El Nino

El Nino in Spanish means 'the boy child' which was traditionally used by Peruvians who fished for anchovy. It describes the appearance of a warm ocean current of the South American coast, adjacent to Peru and Ecuador, around Christmas- hence the reference to the Christ Child. This current temporarily displaces nutrient rich cold water, reducing the food source of the anchovy and, when the warming is exceptionally strong, completely running the anchovy harvest. The changes in oceanic circulation are accompanied by changes in circulation of the air, resulting in altered weather patterns across the globe (Hazardwise, Emergency Management Australia, 1955).

During a normal weather pattern, easterly trade winds bring warm surface water and warm moist air into the western Pacific ocean. This air raises to high levels in atmosphere and travels eastwards before sinking over the eastern Pacific. This is called a normal walker circulation (after Sir Gilbert Walker). In this pattern, the raising air is associated with regions of low pressure and brings soaking rains to Northern and Eastern Australia. The sinking air is associated with high pressure and dry conditions.

During El Nino episodes the walker circulation weakens. This is the result of a region of low pressure developing in the central Pacific, so that easterly trade winds are replaced with westerly winds. Warm water and associated moist air, is pushed by these winds towards South America. The amount of moisture reaching Australia/Asia is therefore reduced, leading to drier conditions and possibly drought.

Thus, two-thirds of the Indian sub-continent comes under arid and semi-arid region and dry sub-humid conditions and is prone to recurrent droughts. The coastal region is frequently affected by cyclones in the summer months of May and June and in October and November. Around 56 per cent of the area is susceptible to seismic disturbances. The Himalayan region and the north-eastern parts are highly unstable and hence subject to severe earthquakes. The 1993 earthquake of Maharashtra reveals that the peninsular India is also under threat of modest to severe earthquake disturbances. Over 40 million hectares of area in the country experiences periodic floods. The country's hilly region is prone to landslides and the Himalayan region to avalanches.

From the above discussion it is evident that the hypotheses no. 1 stating that "there are certain natural disasters which recur regularly in India" has been realised. Thus, it is established that the objective no. 1- 'to list out the disasters that occur in India with a natural trigger' is achieved.

Administration of the Questionnaire and Collection of Data

Sixty eight questionnaire in the suggestive form are mailed to experts in the field of disaster management. Similarly, seventy seven questionnaires in the direct form and in second person parts of speech are sent by mail to the field personnel and students. They are asked for an early return of the duly filled in questionnaires in the enclosed self-addressed envelope meant for the purpose.

The questionnaires were received through mail by the investigator. The response was poor and inspite of the repeated requests and re-mailing of the self-addressed envelopes, only a few were received back. The details are shown in the table 3.5.

Table 3.5: Details of the Questionnaire Mailed and Received

Mode of administration *Category of the sample*	*Mailed*	*Received*
Experts	Sixty eight	Nine
Field personnel and students	Seventy seven	Fifteen

Nine questionnaires in the expert's category and fifteen questionnaires in the field personnel and student's category were received and the investigator used these questionnaires only for analysing the data.

The scoring of the questionnaires, analysis of the scores and inferences drawn from it are given in the fourth chapter.

4

DATA ANALYSIS AND INFERENCES

This chapter discusses the scoring procedure, statistical tests adopted for data analysis, and finalisation of behavioural traits essential for facing the disasters successfully. Besides this, activities for the development of behaviours, their evaluation and inferences drawn are described.

Scoring Procedure

The questionnaires are scored in the manner given below:

The + (plus) point is given for acceptance because it gives a strength to the inclusion of this behaviour in the list of essential traits in meeting the disasters. On the other hand, a N (neutral) point is given for an undecidedness as it neither confirms nor rejects the essentiality of the trait in meeting the disasters. Similarly, a – (minus) point is counted for non-acceptance since it indicates the non-essentiality of this trait in the times of disasters. Thus, the final score of the individual is in terms of number of pluses, minuses and neutrals.

The responses of experts and field personnel/students (henceforth referred to as field personnel only for convenience) as frequencies were scored in terms of pluses, minuses and neutrals as described above and is shown in the Table 4.1.

Table 4.1: Consolidated Scores of Experts and Field Personnel

Item No.	Experts (N = 9)			Field Personnel (N = 15)		
	Plus	Neutral	Minus	Plus	Neutral	Minus
1	1	8	0	11	04	00
2	4	5	0	11	4	0
3	3	4	2	7	7	1
4	5	2	2	14	0	1
5	7	2	0	14	0	1
6	3	1	5	9	3	3
7	9	0	0	14	1	0
8	7	2	0	14	1	0
9	9	0	0	13	1	1
10	3	2	4	12	2	1
11	2	0	7	8	0	7
12	2	3	4	12	2	1
13	7	0	2	14	0	1
14	3	2	4	12	1	2
15	2	1	6	7	0	8
16	3	3	3	7	6	2
17	6	2	1	9	5	1
18	7	2	0	10	4	1
19	6	2	1	13	0	2
20	7	1	1	15	0	0
21	9	0	0	15	0	0
22	2	1	6	3	3	9
23	7	2	0	14	1	0
24	7	2	0	10	5	0
25	8	0	1	15	0	0
26	7	0	2	11	2	2
27	5	4	0	9	5	1
28	8	1	0	15	0	0

Item No.	*Experts (N = 9)*			*Field Personnel (N = 15)*		
	Plus	*Neutral*	*Minus*	*Plus*	*Neutral*	*Minus*
29	8	0	1	15	0	0
30	4	5	0	11	1	3
31	6	0	3	9	4	2
32	5	2	2	1	10	3
33	3	5	1	10	5	0
34	6	3	0	11	4	0
35	3	1	5	9	1	5
36	3	2	4	7	3	5
37	6	3	0	13	2	0
38	3	6	0	15	0	0
39	0	0	9	6	0	9
40	5	4	0	13	2	0
41	7	0	2	13	0	2
42	9	0	0	15	0	0
43	2	6	1	3	6	6
44	1	5	3	5	4	6
45	6	1	2	14	1	0
46	2	3	4	6	6	3
47	4	5	0	7	7	1
48	4	4	1	6	4	5
49	1	3	5	4	9	2
50	6	3	0	11	4	0
51	7	2	0	13	2	0
52	6	3	0	13	1	1
53	6	0	3	10	4	1
54	5	0	4	12	1	2
55	5	0	4	8	1	6
56	5	1	3	11	3	1
57	9	0	0	15	0	0
58	5	4	0	11	4	0

Item No.	Experts (N = 9)			Field Personnel (N = 15)		
	Plus	Neutral	Minus	Plus	Neutral	Minus
59	6	1	2	10	4	1
60	6	1	2	6	4	5
61	7	2	0	14	1	0
62	5	0	4	9	3	3
63	7	1	1	10	2	3
64	6	1	2	15	0	0
65	6	2	1	13	1	1
66	9	0	0	14	1	0
67	4	2	3	6	2	7
68	9	0	0	14	1	0
69	8	0	1	12	3	0
70	8	1	0	8	7	0
71	5	4	0	11	4	0
72	8	1	0	12	1	2
73	5	0	4	10	0	5
74	8	1	0	14	1	0
75	7	1	1	10	0	5
76	3	1	5	7	5	3
77	6	1	2	19	5	0
78	7	0	2	10	3	2
79	4	3	2	10	5	0
80	6	2	1	14	1	0
81	9	0	0	15	0	0
82	9	0	0	15	0	0
83	5	3	1	10	0	5
84	8	0	1	12	2	1
85	5	3	1	12	2	1
86	8	1	0	15	0	0
87	8	1	0	14	1	0
38	6	2	1	11	4	0
89	7	1	1	12	3	0
90	6	1	2	8	1	6

Statistical Analysis

The frequencies of the table 4.1 were subjected to chi-square test for establishing the significance of the obtained responses. For example, the chi-square value calculated for item no. 50 in the field personnel category is shown below in table 4.2.

Table 4.2: Calculation of Chi-square Value for Item no. 50 for the Field Personnel

	Plus	Neutral	Minus
Observed (f_o)	11	4	0
Expected (f_e)	5	5	5
$f_o - f_e$	6	1	5
Correction* (-.5)	5.5	.5	4.5
$(f_o - f_e)^2$	30.25	.25	20.25
$(f_o - f_e)^2/f_e$	30.25/5	.25/5	20.25/5

x2 = E $[(f_o - f_e)^2/f_e]$

= 6.05 + .05 + 4.05 = 10.15 *(Garrett, 1985).

Similarly, the chi-square values for other items and for experts were calculated.

Thus, the chi-square values for all the 90 items with respect to experts and filed personnel were calculated separately and are reported for comparison in table 4.3.

It is clear from the table that some items are significant at both levels that is 0.05 and 0.01 for both experts and field personnel while some other items are non-significant for both experts and field personnel and still other items are significant at 0.05 or 0.01 level either for experts or field personnel only.

The behavioural traits which were significant at least at 0.05 level for both experts and field personnel are pooled together to be used for further study and are shown in table 4.4.

Table 4.3: Chi-square Values of Experts and Field Personnel

Behavioural Trait	Item No.	Chi-square values			
		Experts (N=9)	Significance	Field Personnel (N=15)	Significance
Adjustment	50	4.166	NS	10.15	0.01
	54	2.916	NS	12.15	0.01
	73	2.916	NS	8.1	0.05
	81	14.249	0.01	26.15	0.01
Affection & Friendliness	47	2.916	NS	3.35	NS
	51	6.249	0.05	16.55	0.01
	77	2.916	NS	8.1	0.05
	88	2.916	NS	10.15	0.01
Alertness	25	9.583	0.01	26.15	0.01
	72	9.583	0.01	12.95	0.01
	76	1.5	NS	0.9	NS
	80	2.916	NS	20.95	0.01
	90	2.916	NS	3.75	0.01
Altruism	30	2.916	NS	8.95	0.05
	56	1.5	NS	8.95	0.05
	64	2.916	NS	26.15	0.01
	74	9.583	0.01	20.95	0.01
	86	9.583	0.01	26.15	0.01
Co-operation	24	6.249	0.05	8.1	0.05
	39	14.249	0.01	6.55	0.05
	65	2.916	NS	16.15	0.01
	70	9.583	0.01	5.75	NS
Co-ordination	31	4.166	NS	3.75	NS
	42	14.249	0.01	26.15	0.01
	57	14.249	0.01	26.15	0.01
	85	1.5	NS	12.15	0.01
Courage	1	9.583	0.01	10.15	0.01
	15	2.916	NS	5.75	0.05
	69	9.583	0.01	12.95	0.01
	75	5.583	NS	8.1	0.05

(Chi-square values at 0.05 level is 5.991 & at 0.01 level is 9.210)

Behavioural Trait	Item No.	Chi-square values			
		Experts (N=9)	Significance	Field Personnel (N=15)	Significance
Decision-making ability	9	14.249	0.01	16.15	0.01
	13	6.249	0.05	20.95	0.01
	68	14.249	0.01	20.95	0.01
	89	5.583	NS	12.95	0.01
Empathy	10	0.166	NS	12.15	0.01
	16	0.0	NS	1.75	NS
	48	0.916	NS	0.1	NS
	67	0.166	NS	1.75	NS
Enthusiasm	2	2.916	NS	10.15	0.01
	3	0.166	NS	3.35	NS
	33	1.5	NS	8.1	0.05
	37	4.166	NS	16.55	0.01
	66	14.249	0.01	20.95	0.01
Helpfulness	11	6.249	0.05	5.75	NS
	14	0.166	NS	12.15	0.01
	20	5.583	NS	26.15	0.01
	44	1.5	NS	0.1	NS
	49	1.5	NS	3.75	NS
Independent Thinking	6	1.5	NS	3.35	NS
	41	6.249	0.05	16.55	0.01
	45	2.916	NS	20.95	0.01
	53	4.166	NS	6.55	0.05
	55	2.916	NS	3.75	NS
Initiative	12	0.166	NS	12.15	0.01
	21	14.249	0.01	26.15	0.01
	28	9.583	0.01	26.15	0.01
	58	2.916	NS	10.15	0.01
Leadership	4	0.916	NS	20.95	0.01
	8	6.249	0.05	20.95	0.01
	34	4.166	NS	10.15	0.01
	46	0.166	NS	0.55	NS
	83	1.5	NS	8.1	0.05

(Contd...)

Behavioural Trait	*Item No.*	*Chi-square values*			
		Experts (N=9)	*Signi-ficance*	*Field Personnel (N=15)*	*Signi-ficance*
Rationality	23	6.249	0.05	20.95	0.01
	27	2.916	NS	4.9	NS
	59	2.916	NS	6.55	0.05
	82	14.249	0.01	26.15	0.01
	87	9.583	0.01	20.95	0.01
Realism	22	2.916	NS	3.35	NS
	26	6.249	0.05	8.55	0.05
	43	2.916	NS	0.55	NS
	60	2.916	NS	0.1	NS
	71	2.916	NS	10.15	0.01
Sharing	38	4.166	NS	26.15	0.01
	52	4.166	NS	16.15	0.01
	61	6.249	0.05	20.95	0.01
	78	6.249	0.05	5.75	NS
Spontaneity	5	6.249	0.05	20.95	0.01
	17	2.916	NS	4.9	NS
	32	0.916	NS	6.55	0.05
	62	2.916	NS	3.35	NS
	79	0.166	NS	8.1	0.05
Sportsmanship	19	2.916	NS	16.55	0.01
	36	0.166	NS	0.9	NS
	40	2.916	NS	16.55	0.01
	63	5.583	NS	5.75	NS
	84	9.583	0.01	12.16	0.01
Sympathy	7	14.249	0.01	20.95	0.01
	18	6.249	0.05	6.55	0.05
	29	9.583	0.01	26.15	0.01
	35	1.5	NS	4.9	NS

(where NS - Non-significant)

The table 4.4 shows that all items except the items 39 and 1 have positive responses outnumbering the neutral and negative responses for both experts and field personnel.

Table 4.4: Consolidated Scores of Experts and Field Personnel which are Significant at Least 0.05 Level

Behavioural trait	*Item No.*	*Experts (N=9)*			*Field Personnel (N=15)*		
		Plus	*Neutral*	*Minus*	*Plus*	*Neutral*	*Minus*
Adjustment	81	9	0	0	15	0	0
Affection and Friendliness	51	7	2	0	13	2	0
Alertness	25	8	0	1	15	0	0
	72	8	1	0	12	3	0
Altruism	74	8	1	0	14	1	0
	86	8	1	0	15	0	0
Co-operation	24	7	2	0	10	5	0
	39	0	0	9	6	0	9
Co-ordination	42	9	0	0	15	0	0
	57	9	0	0	15	0	0
Courage	1	1	8	0	11	4	0
	69	8	0	1	12	3	0
Decision-making ability	9	9	0	0	13	1	1
	13	7	0	2	14	0	1
	68	9	0	0	14	1	0

Table 4.4: Contd.

Behavioural trait	*Item No.*	*Experts (N=9)*			*Field Personnel (N=15)*		
		Plus	*Neutral*	*Minus*	*Plus*	*Neutral*	*Minus*
Enthusiasm	66	9	0	0	14	1	0
Independent thinking	41	7	0	2	13	0	2
Initiative	21	9	0	0	15	0	0
	28	8	1	0	15	0	0
Leadership	8	7	2	0	14	1	0
Rationality	23	7	2	0	14	1	0
	82	9	0	0	15	0	0
	87	8	1	0	14	1	0
Realism	26	7	0	2	11	2	2
Sharing	61	7	2	0	14	1	0
Spontaneity	5	7	2	0	14	1	0
Sportsmanship	84	8	0	1	12	2	1
Sympathy	7	9	0	0	14	1	0
	18	7	2	0	10	4	1
	29	8	0	1	15	0	0

Item no. 39 elicited 9 negative responses from experts and 6 positive responses and 9 negative responses from field personnel. Whereas item no. 1 elicited 1 positive and 8 neutral responses from experts and 11 positive and 4 neutral responses from the field personnel.

Item no. 39 which assesses the aspect of working together for the common purpose (i.e., co-operation) failed to elicit the expected response as per the pilot study conducted and discussed on page no... The weightage given by the individuals stresses more on the second part of the negative alternate i.e., "........... work better" inspite of negative response for the originally thought over direction. Because of the dichotomy between the responses of the pilot study and actual study, the inclusion of this item is deferred and ultimately dropped after substantial discussion from including for further study.

Item no. 1 assessing the aspect of boldness (i.e., courage) failed to elicit the expected response as per the pilot study conducted and described on page no... The weightage given by the experts stresses more on the "...... take all possible preventive measures.......... and leave it to God". The item provides positive direction partially and inspite of the dichotomy that existed between experts and field personnel, this item is retained for further study.

In gist, only one item i.e., item no. 39 'co-operation' has been dropped and all the remaining 29 items have been considered valid. Thus, it is concluded from the data analysis that the behavioural traits essential for a person to meet the disaster situations are:

(i) Adjustment, the item no. 81 assessing the aspect of 'regulate';

(ii) Affection and Friendliness, item no. 51 assessing the aspect of 'expressing kind feeling';

(iii) Alertness, assessing of 'look-out against danger' and 'watchful' aspects with item no. 25 and 72 respectively;

(iv) Altruism, the item no. 74 and 86 assessing the 'well-being' and 'happiness of others first and unselfishness' aspects, respectively;

(v) Co-operation, the item no. 24 assessing the aspect of 'working together for common purpose';

(vi) Co-ordination, assessing the aspect of 'cause to function together' with items 42 and 57;

(vii) Courage, with item no.1 assessing 'boldness' and item no. 69, 'brave enough to do what one feels right';

(viii) Decision-making ability, assessing the aspect of 'judging' with item no. 9 and 68, while 'to decide and act accordingly' with item no. 13;

(ix) Enthusiasm, the item no. 66 assessing the aspect of 'strong feeling of admiration or interest';

(x) Independent thinking, assessing the aspect of 'unwilling to be under the obligation to others', with item no. 41;

(xi) Initiative, item no. 21 and 28, assessing the aspects of 'ability to act without being prompted by others' and 'capacity to see what needs to be done and enterprise enough to do it', respectively;

(xii) Leadership, assessing the aspect of 'giving person a lead', with item no. 8;

(xiii) Rationality, the aspect of 'ability to reason' is assessed by items 23, 62 and 87;

(xiv) Realism, item no. 26 assessing the aspect of 'being practical';

(xv) Sharing, the aspect of 'enduring jointly with others' assessed with item no. 61;

(xvi) Spontaneity, assessing the aspect of 'happening from natural impulse with item no. 5;

(xvii) Sportsmanship, the aspect of 'willing to take risks and is not downheartened, if lost, is assessed by item no. 84;

(xviii) Sympathy, has the aspects of 'capacity for being simultaneously affected with the same feeling as another', 'tendency to share another person's emotion or sensation or condition' and 'mental participation with another in his trouble or with another's trouble' assessed through items 7, 18 and 29 respectively.

The above tables and discussion show that the hypotheses no. 2 stating that "certain behavioural traits are essential to meet disaster situations" has been realised. Thus, it is established that the objective no.2, that is, 'to establish behavioural traits essential to meet natural disaster situations' is achieved.

Development of Activities

The classroom activities for the development of behavioural traits essential to meet disaster situations were developed through review of books and International Decade for Natural Disaster Reduction publications, and brain-storming sessions with the supervisor, the research scholars and the investigator. This exercise was done to gain information about the third objective, i.e., 'to develop the curricular activities at primary school level for developing the behaviours necessary to meet the disaster situations.

The investigator held brain-storming sessions, each of half-an-hour duration with research scholars only with research scholars and supervisor together and with supervisor only. The number of brain-storming sessions taken for the development of activities for the behaviours is shown in table 4.5.

Table 4.5: Brain-storming Sessions and the Behavioural Traits

Sl.No.	*Behavioural trait*	*Investigator and Research Scholars*	*Investigator, Research Scholars and Supervisor*	*Investigator and Supervisor*
1.	Adjustment	one	two	nil
2.	Affection and Friendliness	one	three	nil
3.	Alertness	one	three	one
4.	Altruism	two	one	one
5.	Co-operation	one	two	one
6.	Co-ordination	one	one	one
7.	Courage	two	two	nil
8.	Decision-making ability	one	one	one
9.	Enthusiasm	one	one	nil
10.	Independent thinking	two	two	two
11.	Initiative	one	two	one
12.	Leadership	one	one	one
13.	Rationality	one	two	two
14.	Realism	one	one	one
15.	Sharing	one	one	one
16.	Spontaneity	one	nil	one
17.	Sportsmanship	one	two	nil
18.	Sympathy	two	two	nil
	Total	twenty two	twenty eight	fourteen

The table 4.5 shows that in all (22+28+14=64) sixty four brain-storming sessions were held by the investigator with research scholars and supervisor.

While developing the activities, it is kept in mind that the:

(a) material required should be available indigenously

(b) activity is cost effective

(c) activity is child-friendly

(d) activity is easily comprehendable

(e) constituent aspects of the behavioural trait.

Keeping these points in view, the activities are developed for each of the essential behavioural traits as explained below:

Adjustment

Adjustment comprises of the aspects of 'regulating the things'.

For initiating adjustment, the activities that were planned to be introduced in the classroom are as follows:

1. Teacher draws a 4" x 4" square on a paper and cuts. Then, this piece of paper is cut into irregular pieces. Likewise, 10 sets are prepared and each set is given to a student. The students are asked to spread these irregular pieces on a newspaper to get a regular square form and also fit into a square of the paper.

The students attempt to join the ends by their curvature to form a whole and regulate the things –an aspect of 'adjustment'.

Ten students can participate in this activity. On the next occasion, choose shapes of a circle, a hexagon, a rectangle, and so on, with other set of students to cover the whole class.

Thus, 'adjustment' is developed in students.

2. Students are divided into groups of eight each. To the members of a group, the teacher gives one pencil each

to two students, two pencils each to another two students, and does not give any pencil to the others. Teacher asks them to draw a figure and observes whether the students with two pencils share with others who do not have any. The teacher reinforces the positive behaviour.

In this activity, the student who is having excess number of pencils distributes to other students and regulates the things, which is an aspect of 'adjustment'.

This activity can be conducted for eight students. So if the class is larger, this activity can be repeated with other materials such as sketch pens, crayons, books, etc., for drawing, reading, etc., on other occasions.

Affection and Friendliness

The aspect covered for 'affection and friendliness' is showing or expressing kind feeling.

For inculcating affection and friendliness, the activities planned to be introduced in the classroom are as follows:

1. Students are divided into two groups – A and B. In the role-play, the students of group B are asked to scratch the back and move a rubber lizard on the hands of group A members. The students feel the pinch and shout. At this juncture, the teacher poses a question as to what a tree feels when a squirrel runs up the trunk and when it is cut. Students of group A, having felt a strange feeling, answer that the trees feel the scratching and hurt.

   Next time, the roles of groups A and B are reversed.

Thus, the students understand and internalise that the plants and animals are living things like human beings and should not be harmed. This activity develops affection towards other living things.

2. The students are taken on an excursion – a visit to zoo, a visit to a park, a visit to a planetarium, a field

trip to a picnic spot, a field trip to biscuit factory, etc. On their journey, the students interact with each other, such as knowing their names, likes and dislikes, place of residence, names of their friends and siblings, and so on.

This activity develops 'friendliness' in the students because their interaction enables them to come closer and develop affinity towards each other.

Alertness

Alertness has the aspects of 'being watchful' and 'on the look-out against danger, misfortune or attack'.

To initiate alertness the following activities are planned in the classroom:

1. Let the students discuss the weather. How many types of weather conditions can they describe? Ask the students to prepare symbolic drawings of different weather conditions like the ones shown in the figure 4.1:

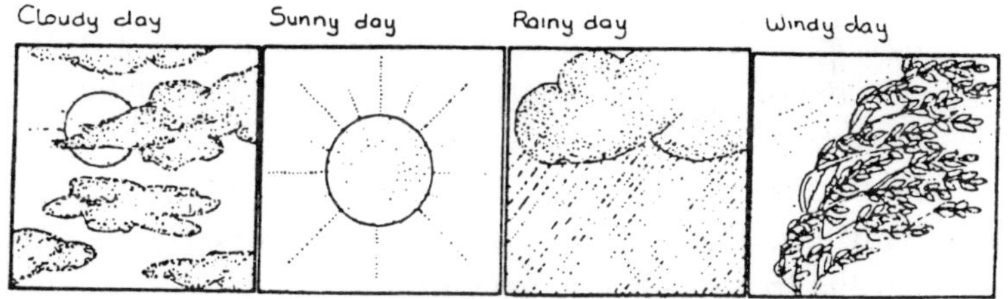

Figure 4.1: Symbolic drawings of different weather conditions.

The students can develop symbols according to the climate in their area.

Students should make a chart with a square of 4 cm. × 4 cm. for each day of the month. They should be asked to fill each of these squares with a symbolic drawing appropriate to the weather prevailing on that day. For example, if the season is monsoon and it is very cloudy on

Monday the 1st, the students will stick the "Very cloudy" grey-coloured symbol on the square. On Tuesday the 2nd, if it is rainy, the students will paste the "Rainy Day" black-coloured umbrella symbol on the square and so on.

Ask the students to make weather predictions each morning as they come to school and to record them. Were they right? If so how many times each month? They could record right or wrong predictions by putting a "v" or "x" in each corner of the day's square alongwith the correct symbol.

Later, ask the students to compare their observations with the weather forecasts in the newspaper brought to the classroom by the teacher or on radio or television at home. (Joy of Learning, Handbook of Environmental Education Activities, 1986)

2. Students are made into groups of nine each. Let the school premises be prepared as a traffic system with cross roads having zebra crossings for pedestrians, signals for pedestrians as well as motorists. A role-play is enacted by the group A students. One student acts as a traffic policeman. Four students cross the road on the zebra crossings when the pedestrian signal is green. Similarly, let two students drive a tricycle, another two students a baby car. They observe traffic signals i.e., red to stop, orange to go slow and green to go.

Traffic signals are used to demonstrate that it is dangerous to cross the road when it is red.

This activity develops 'alertness' in students.

3. A group of 10 students plays a game of musical chairs. The students go around the 9 chairs arranged in a circle. They stop and sit on the chairs when the music stops. As there are only 9 chairs, only 9 students will sit on the chairs and the tenth student who is not able

to secure a seat is viewed as not attentive. Likewise, the game is played upto the last chair and the winner is rewarded.

This activity of musical chairs develops alertness in the students because they are always on the watch.

Altruism

The aspects covered in altruism are 'unselfishness' and 'the principle of considering the well-being and happiness of others first'.

To inculcate 'altruism' the following activities are planned:

1. A two-week old pup is given to each of the two groups of students. They nurture the pups with the food they bring to school.

After three months, the nurturing of two pups is evaluated and the class which reared the pup to a healthy one is reinforced. The healthy pup received more attention, care & food, because of unselfishness of the students.

Further, the reinforcement of one class by the teacher enables the students of other group to review their behaviour and try to be unselfish in future.

'The principle of considering the well-being and happiness of others first' can be developed in the following manner:

During a potluck lunch session, the teacher asks the children to give foodstuffs, first to the neighbours and then feed themselves. In simple terms "Athidhi Devo Bavah".

This activity is repeated, for the children to internalise the aspect of 'considering the well-being and happiness of others first'.

Thus, it is inferred in a general manner that these activities develop altruism in the students.

Co-operation

'Co-operation' has the aspect of 'working together for a common purpose'.

For internalising this behaviour the activities that are planned to be introduced in the classroom are as follows:

1. Let each student be the in-charge of relevant pictures and resources, posters, useful equipment such as magnifying lenses, plaster of paris or dough, pencils, paper, scissors, etc. Each child is responsible to give the material and keep safe after its use. Each student when he is to use the material borrows from another student, that is, if a student is using red pencil, the other student has to use blue pencil. Likewise, when one student cuts paper by using scissors, let that be pasted in a scrap book by another student.

The teacher observes that students use the material one after another and complete the work assigned to one of them.

This activity develops 'co-operation' in the students.

2. The students feel fun to have a small garden of their own. They can grow radishes, greentail onions, lettuce and pumpkins. Let one student get the seeds, another child so them, still another water them. The students will be proud of themselves and would check their plants many times a day. In this activity students work together and it is inferred in a general manner to develop 'co-operation'.

Co-ordination

Co-ordination covers the aspect of 'cause to function together or in proper order'.

For inculcating co-ordination the following activity is planned in the classroom:

Let ten students hold placards with a sentence each of a known story. Ask the students to jumble up. The audience (the remaining students) try to build story in a sequence.

When a student from the audience identifies and reads the first sentence, the student holding the first sentence comes and stands in front of the teacher. Then, another student from the audience spells out the second sentence to make a meaningful story, the student holding the second sentence comes and stands to the left of the first student. Likewise, as students complete the story, one student after another comes in order and stands one besides the other. This exercise develops a sense of 'cause to function in proper order' in the student.

This activity meant for the students of Class III, develops 'co-ordination'.

This activity can be repeated with different groups of students with a different story, if the strength of the class is more than ten.

The same activity can be repeated for Class II students with words forming a proverb/saying/idiom/phrase, etc. and Class I students with letters forming a word.

Courage

Courage has the aspects of 'boldness' and 'brave enough to do what one feels to be right'.

To inculcate 'courage' the activities that are planned to be introduced in the classroom are as follows:

1. In a general manner, the teacher reinforces the student who speaks the truth. This develops 'boldness' in the students as their behaviour is recognised by the teacher and in front of others.
2. Students of Class III are made into groups of 5. One student from Class IV is selected and is asked to lose

the race deliberately when he/she is competing in a running race alongwith one group from Class III. At the end of the competition one student of Class III wins. Thus confidence of the student is reinforced.

The activity is repeated with another student from Class IV with the same instructions and conduct competition along with another group of Class III. Likewise, another student from Class III wins and develops 'braveness'.

In this activity, the students of Class III develop courage to face competitions.

Decision-making Ability

Decision-making ability comprises of the aspects of 'judging' and 'the ability to decide and act accordingly'.

For inculcating the decision-making ability, the activities that are planned to be introduced in the classroom are as follows:

1. A maze problem consisting of a rabbit and a carrot is given to a student. He is asked to find the path for the rabbit to reach the carrot. The student after few trials succeeds in the task.

In this activity, the students considers different paths, of which only one is a correct one, thus, developing the 'judging' ability.

2. The students are made into two groups, A and B, of 5 each. Let group A have 5 toys and decide with respect to its hiding place. Group A students give clues regarding the hiding place to group B to find out the toys. Group B finds out the toys with the help of clues given to them. The teacher encourages the students to hide the toys in various different places.

This activity enables the students to 'decide and act accordingly'. The students of group A decide about the hiding place for toys whereas the group B students decide about locating the toys.

The exercise is then repeated with the roles exchanged. Let group B decide the hiding place for toys and group A find them.

This activity covers ten students at a time. If the strength of the class is more, the activity is repeated.

Enthusiasm

The aspect of 'strong feeling of interest in the activity' is covered in enthusiasm.

To inculcate enthusiasm the activities that are planned to be introduced in the classroom are as follows:

1. Students are made into groups of 5 each. Each group is asked to collect as many stones as possible and bring with them the following day. The teacher collects the coloured stones from the groups and makes a note of it.

This activity can be repeated by telling them to improve the performance further. Likewise, the students try to improve their performance which the teacher reinforces verbally and develops enthusiasm in them.

2. The students are taken to a park where different types of trees are present. Divide the class into groups of four or five and let them settle down in different places. Let the students observe a few trees and recognise the main parts of a tree. Let them practice drawing or sketching the main parts of a tree.

The students can be asked to sketch the shapes of the trees highlighting the positions of the different parts and paste them in a scrap book.

This activity enables the students to maintain interest in plants, thus developing 'enthusiasm' in them.

Independent Thinking

The aspect of 'unwilling to be under the obligation of others' is included in independent thinking.

For inculcating independent thinking the activities that are planned to be introduced in the classroom are as follows:

1. Students are given pieces of paper on which there are lines such as ---, |, L, /, \, V. Teacher asks them to develop pictures over these lines in ten minutes. At the end of the session, the teacher collects the papers and finds many number of pictures. The teacher reinforces the students' efforts.

In this activity, students are neither under the compulsion of the teacher nor taking any guidance from the teacher, but are thinking independently to draw pictures. Thus, they develop 'independent thinking'.

2. Students are made into five groups. The first student in each group is given a separate story comprising of four or five sentences and is asked to give a title to it. Student who gives an appropriate title to the story is reinforced by the teacher.

The activity is repeated with the second, third, fourth, and fifth set of students with different stories on different sessions.

This activity develops 'independent thinking' in students because they do not take anybody's help in giving a title to the story.

Initiative

Initiative includes the aspects of 'an ability to act without being prompted by others' and 'capacity to see what needs to be done and enterprise enough to do it'.

For instituting initiative the activities planned in the classroom are given below:

1. The students are shown a different drawing or painting technique, at least once a week. How the medium works – with water and without water, on different papers, to make a misty picture, a watery picture and so on is demonstrated. Students follow what the teacher does and in addition have an opportunity to explore the media for themselves. They often have their own ideas for techniques.

The students are encouraged and helped to display pieces of their own work or models in an interesting and aesthetic way on a display board. They learn to mount two dimensional works with borders and place models on their own display mats. Appropriate labels are added later.

In this activity the students 'act without being prompted by others' as demonstrated in the work of their display.

2. Students were divided into groups of 5 each. To the Group A, the teacher shows a series of pictures related to a 'thirsty crow' as shown in the figure 4.2.

Figure 4.2: Pictures related to the 'thirsty crow'

The students are asked to describe the pictures. According to the them, the 1st picture shows – a crow was very thirsty; 2nd picture – it wandered here and there for water and at last saw a water pot near a well; 3rd picture – it looked inside the pot. There was very little water in the pot; 4th picture – it saw some stones near the well.

The students are asked the manner in which the crow quenches its thirst. After analysing the situation, one student replies that the crow picks up some stones, puts them one by one into the pot, the water level comes up and the crow drinks water.

This activity enables the students 'to see what needs to be done & enterprise enough to do it'.

The activity is repeated for other students and also with different problem situations.

Thus, 'initiative' is developed in the students.

Leadership

'Giving person a lead' is an aspect of leadership.

For inculcating leadership the activities that are planned to be introduced in the classroom are given below:

Let the students be divided into groups of 3 each. The teacher takes the students of the first group and asks them to stand in a line – one behind the other. The teacher stands in front of the first group and asks the students to hold the dress of the student in front so as to form a link.

The teacher demonstrates the game of a train wherein he/she is the engine and the students behind act as compartments and go around and inside the classroom alongwith the teacher.

After a few minutes the teacher leaves the first group alone, and asks the students of all the groups including the first group to stand one behind the other. The teacher asks the students who are in the front in each group to act as engines and the others follow them around and inside the classroom.

Later, the teacher asks the students to exchange their roles so as to see that each student in a group to gets an opportunity to lead the members. This activity develops the ability to 'give them a lead' – an aspect of 'leadership'.

Rationality

'The ability of reasoning' is covered in rationality.

For internalising 'rationality', the activities that are planned are as follows:

1. Let groups of two students play a see-saw one on each side. Another student joins him and sits on one side. Then the opposite side which has one student goes up. Ask them why it happens so.

The student gives reason as to why it goes up. The side which has one student goes up because the weight on that side is less than the opposite side which has two students. Thus, explaining the phenomenon in a rational manner depicts rationality.

2. Let the students play 'tug of war game'-three versus five. The group which has five students wins the game.

The students are asked why the group of five students won the game. They give reason that the group of five which is larger than a group of three, has more strength and so it won.

This activity develops 'rationality'.

Realism

The aspect included in realism is 'being practical'.

For inculcating realism the activity planned to be introduced in the classroom is as follows:

The students are given the mutilated toys, say, a duck with a broken limb, a car with two wheels, etc. alongwith clay. They are asked to prepare models.

Even before they replicate the toys, students try to mend the mutilated toys to make it a whole. Then, students prepare exactly the same type of clay models as they see from the given mutilated toys.

Students who replicate the model as given in the mutilated toys have developed 'realism' because they are practical with regard to the thing or situation that is described or the representation of familiar things as they really are.

Sharing

The aspects of 'giving away part of' and 'enduring jointly with others' are covered in the sharing.

Sharing can be instituted by the classroom activities planned as discussed below:

1. Everyday during the lunch session, let the students have a common sharing lunch. Each student gives a portion of his foodstuff to others, who in turn give portion of their's to still others.

The teacher reinforces the appropriate behaviour by involving themselves in the activity.

In this activity there is 'giving away a part of what a person possesses' and hence, it develops the 'sharing'.

2. During the occasions of school functions, national and religious festivals, let the students be made into groups of five each. Then, they are allotted the work of keeping the classroom surroundings clean and green. Group A members are asked to pick up small stones, bits of paper and other unwanted material from inside and outside the classroom. Group B members hold the broomstick and sweep the floor for cleaning. Next,

Group C members cut the colour papers, make different shapes from coloured paper and decorate the classroom.

Likewise, this activity can be conducted for 15 students at a time. If the strength of the class is more than 15, then the activity is repeated with other students on a different occasion.

This activity provides them to 'endure jointly the hardships and fruits of the work' turned out by the students. Thus, endurance in 'sharing' with others is developed in the students.

Spontaneity

The aspect covered in spontaneity is 'happening from a natural impulse'.

To internalise spontaneity the classroom activities planned are given below:

1. Letters of the alphabet are written separately on small pieces of paper, rolled and placed in a small jar. The teacher asks the students to pick up a paper, spell out as many words starting with that alphabet, as he can in one minute. The teacher notes down the words of the student. Similarly, another student picks up another alphabet and spells out words and the teacher makes a note of it. Likewise ten students are asked to continue with the activity. At the end of the activity, the teacher reinforces the students by repeating their words and the student who spelt maximum words is given a small gift (a pencil, an eraser, a crayon, a book, etc.,).

If the students are many in number, then the activity is repeated in another session with other students.

In this activity, students are responding naturally on the spot and trying to give maximum number of words in the prescribed time limit. Thus, the behaviour 'spontaneity' will be developed in them.

2. Plaster of paris, dough, clay and other moulding material is placed in the classroom. Each student is asked to prepare as many number of objects as possible of his choice in fifteen minutes from the given material.

At the end of fifteen minutes, students prepare objects such as a stick, a plate, a ball, a rat, a bat, and so on from different materials. The teacher reinforces the student's efforts in preparing the objects and the student who prepared the maximum number of objects is given a small gift (a pencil, a scale, a crayon, a book, etc.,).

As the students respond spontaneously to prepare maximum number of objects from the given moulding material in the prescribed time limit, they develop 'spontaneity' behaviour.

Sportsmanship

Sportsmanship has the aspect of 'willing to take risks and is not down-heartened, if lost'.

To inculcate 'sportsmanship' the activity planned to be introduced in the classroom is given on the next page.

In a simulated condition five tasks of increasing difficulty are presented to the students. Say, a student is able to do all the tasks successfully, another student completes 4 tasks, still another 3 tasks, and so on and so forth.

The teacher reinforces the student who performed 3 tasks successfully and develops in them the urge to perform all the 5 tasks in the next session. Similarly, a student who performed all the tasks successfully interacts with a student who is able to do 3 tasks and builds confidence in him.

Likewise, the teacher reinforcement and the successful students interaction with the students of lesser performance will improve the latter's performance in the next session.

In this activity, the successful students look upon and interact with the less performed and also the latter develop tolerance and strive hard to succeed.

Thus, the aspect of 'willing to take risks and is not down-heartened, if lost', is developed in the students.

Sympathy

Sympathy covers the aspects of 'capacity for being simultaneously affected with the same feeling as another'; 'tendency to share another person's emotion'; and 'mental participation with another in his trouble'.

For internalising sympathy the activity planned to be introduced in the classroom is as follows:

Let students form pairs. One in each pair is blind-folded and each pair is asked to walk through a series of obstacles like a ditch, tree or an overhanging branch with the partner who can see, leading. If obstacles are not available, these can be created with marks on the ground, posting volunteers to be trees, or using furniture (Joy of Learning, Handbook of Environmental Education Activities, 1986).

The partner who leads should do so without talking, by taking the hand of his blind-folded partner and makes him feel the obstacles and difficulties the blind face in the daily life situations. This develops sympathetic feeling in the students.

After a while, the roles in each pair should be reversed. This activity can be conducted for ten students. If the strength is more, the activity is repeated a number of times on different days.

This activity of leading the blind involves 'capacity for being simultaneously affected with the same feeling as another' at the time of reversing the roles, where the student who led is blind-folded later; whereas 'tendency to share another person's emotion' at the time of feeling pain due to obstructions or falling down; and 'mental participation with another in his trouble' when the student who is leading interacts and guides the blind-folded. Thus, the activity develops 'sympathy'.

Evaluation of the Activities

The activities were conducted in Sri Vani Kindergarten and Primary School, Dilsukhnagar, Hyderabad, because of the close association and courteous behaviour exhibited by the management.

The details of the number of exposures for the appearance of the various behavioural traits and the corresponding mode of evaluation adopted by the investigator is shown in the table 4.6.

As shown in the fourth column of the table 4.6, the mode of evaluation was used and the realisation of the appropriate behavioural trait was established. A number of exposures as required for the children to the activities described earlier in order to exhibit the behavioural trait. Finally, only when the investigator is satisfied, it is concluded that the expected behavioural trait has been precipitated in the child. The details are provided in the following paragraphs:

For the evaluation of 'adjustment' the students were taken to the adjacent room which accommodates less number than the original room. Four students sat on the bench where previously it used to accommodate three comfortably. The students adjusted themselves and did not complain of the lack of seating arrangement. Hence, it is inferred from observation that the students acquired the 'adjustment'.

Affection and friendliness is evaluated through observation. The kindness to living things and their

Table 4.6: Number of Exposures for the Appearance of the Behavioural Traits and their Mode of Evaluation

Sl.No.	*Behavioural trait*	*Number of exposures for the appearance*	*Mode of evaluation*
1.	Adjustment	16	Observation
2.	Affection and friendliness	14	Observation
3.	Alertness	17	Observation
4.	Altruism	18	Observation
5.	Co-operation	16	Observation
6.	Co-ordination	14	Observation
7.	Courage	18	Discussion
8.	Decision-making ability	16	Discussion
9.	Enthusiasm	15	Observation
10.	Independent thinking	16	Discussion
11.	Initiative	18	Observation
12.	Leadership	17	Observation
13.	Rationality	17	Discussion
14.	Realism	18	Observation
15.	Sharing	14	Observation
16.	Spontaneity	17	Discussion
17.	Sportsmanship	16	Observation
18.	Sympathy	16	Simulation

relationship with plants and animals is observed to infer this behavioural trait.

Alertness is evaluated by observing the students practising the traffic rules in real life situations i.e., near their school.

Altruism is observed in the situations where the students give a small food item to an old lady sitting near the school gate.

The co-operative behaviour is observed during the students birthday parties where they take up different roles for the success of the occasion.

Co-ordination is evaluated by observing the students ability to speak or present the ideas coherently during an elocution competition.

Courage is evaluated by discussing with the student during which he/she is free to express his/her ideas boldly.

For the evaluation of 'decision making ability' the plan to complete a task is discussed and then it is observed if it is executed in the manner planned earlier.

'Enthusiasm' is observed in the activity of collecting the photographs of the Indian heroes of freedom struggle.

For the evaluation of 'independent thinking' discussion about the student's capability of solving the riddles and puzzles are taken up.

Initiative is observed in an activity where the student is the first person to take action or tell a story.

Leadership is observed during a field-trip to a zoological or botanical garden at the time of taking lunch or getting down from the bus or maintaining discipline.

For evaluating 'rationality' the reasons for not being able to move and walk immediately after playing merry-go-round is discussed.

Realism is observed during a drawing session where the student is able to draw a picture similar to the one that is being given, inspite of its incompleteness.

'Sharing' is evaluated by observing the students in the completion of the project such as a model of zoological garden, himalayas, railway station and bus station.

Spontaneity is evaluated by discussing the various possible uses of a common thing like paper so as to elicit maximum number of ideas in the prescribed time.

The competitions of running a race or lemon-and-spoon race enabled to observe the persons with sportsmanship spirit who did not bother about winning the race but their emphasis was on having fun.

Sympathy is evaluated in a simulated condition, the shared feelings of the students towards two elderly persons who narrate their woes of being stranded in a flood.

For each of the above behaviours to get formulated, on an average, it took sixteen sittings or enactment of the activity for sixteen times.

The activities that took eighteen exposures were for the behavioural traits 'altruism', 'courage', 'initiative', and 'realism' while the remaining only fourteen exposures for the appearance of the expected behavioural trait for which the activity was planned.

The behavioural traits were checked by simulation, discussion and observation. This process of assessing the appearance of the behaviour in the children was started after the tenth exposure of the activity concerned. Except the behaviours 'altruism', 'courage', 'initiative', and 'realism' all others appeared in the students after the tenth exposure.

From the above discussion, it could be concluded that the activity should be repeated at least fourteen times and for the best results eighteen times during the tenure of the children in their pursuit of primary school education.

The above tables and discussion reveal that that the hypothes is no. 3 which states that "the essential behavioural traits to meet disaster situations can be developed through classroom activities at the primary school level" has been realised. Thus, the objective no. 3, that is, 'to suggest the curricular activities at primary school level' for developing the behavioural traits essential to meet the disaster situations.

The details of the incorporation of these activities in the existing curriculum is discussed in the fifth chapter.

5

INTERPRETATION OF DATA

This chapter is totally concerned with revamping the existing curriculum. This aspect helps in realising the fourth objective – 'to incorporate the developed activities in the existing curriculum'.

Components to Consider in Developing a Curriculum

Curriculum deals with content and teaching and learning experiences. All curriculum contents, that is facts, concepts, generalisations and so on – enable students to gain understanding and to apply that understanding to daily living – present and anticipated (Ornstein & Hunkins, 1988).

Curriculum planners consider a psychological organisation as a means to denote the way an individual might actually learn a subject. The content has to be organised by going from the students' immediate environment to a more distant environment, i.e., the concrete content is experienced first, then the more abstract. Thus, psychological factor is a key principle of sequencing content.

The investigator feels that developing a separate course or programme for the above activities and asking the teachers to implement the same in schools may or may not be practicable. Consequently, it may generate some kind of antagonism for its receptivity. Hence, it is felt that, it is necessary to amalgamate the prepared activities at some appropriate place in the existing curriculum so that the workload of teachers is not affected.

The existing curriculum was probed for identifying appropriate slots to introduce the activities that have been finalised.

The Content Analysis of Text-books for Behavioural Traits and Incorporation of the Activities

The content analysis is made by noting down the terms/ words/meanings/situations revealing the aspects of the essential behavioural traits to be used during the disaster situations. Interestingly, majority of the activities could be accommodated through manoeuvring the content that is already existing at present in the primary school curriculum.

Adjustment

The content for the behavioural trait 'adjustment' found in the books is shown in the table 5.1.

Table 5.1. Content Analysis for the Behavioural Trait 'Adjustment'

Subject & Class		*Page no.*	*Related content in the form of terms/words/ meanings/situations*
Hindi B	III	44	. . . . सब कुछ सहती हूँ
Soc. Std.	I	24	Keep everything in the proper place.
	II	23	It is good to drink water with sugar and a pinch of salt during hot summer.
		24	Use umbrellas and raincoats during rainy season. Wear woollen clothes to keep warm.
		49	Municipality arranges to clean our surroundings, roads and markets.
	III	50	Air-conditioning apparatus
Science	I	30	Stables must be kept clean.
	II	40	Ventilators let out foul air.
	III	13	Put the instruments in proper place after use.
		15	Collect glass pieces with a thick cloth and put them carefully in a dustbin.

(where B denotes Hindi Bharati, Soc. Std. denotes Social studies)

The content described above relates to 'adjustment' in different subjects at Classes I, II and III. The teacher can incorporate the activities suggested by the investigator under each behavioural trait as described earlier in day-to-day teaching. As is described on page no...., the activities were developed on the basis of various aspects of the behavioural traits. Hence, while incorporating the activities it is essential to consider these constituents of the behavioural traits.

For example, while teaching the content of page number 24 of Class II Social studies, i.e., "Use umbrellas and raincoats during rainy season. Wear woollen clothes to keep warm", the teacher can take up any one of the following activities to inculcate the aspects of 'adjustment'. The details are shown below:

1. Teacher draws a 4" × 4" square on a paper and cuts. Then, this piece of paper is cut into irregular pieces. Likewise, 10 sets are prepared and each set is given to a student. The students are asked to spread these irregular pieces on a newspaper to get a regular square form and also fit into a square of the paper.

The students attempt to join the ends by their curvature to form a whole and regulate the things – an aspect of 'adjustment'.

Ten students can participate in this activity. On the next occasion, choose shapes of a circle, a hexagon, a rectangle, and so on, with other set of students to cover the whole class.

2. Students are divided into groups of eight each. To the members of a group, the teacher gives one pencil each to two students, two pencils each to another two students, and does not give any pencil to the others. The teacher asks them to draw a figure and observes whether the students with two pencils share with

others who do not have any. The teacher reinforces the positive behaviour.

In this activity, the student who is having excess number of pencils distributes to other students and regulates the things which is an aspect of 'adjustment'.

This activity can be conducted for eight students. So, if the class is larger, this activity can be repeated with other materials such as sketch pens, crayons, books, etc., for drawing, reading, etc., on other occasions.

Affection and Friendliness

The content for 'affection and friendliness' found in the text-books is given in the following the table 5.2.

Table 5.2. Content Analysis for Affection and Friendliness

Subject & Class		*Page no.*	*Related content in form of terms/words/ meanings/situations*
English	I	54	Monkeys were friendly with the squirrel.
		57	Be polite. You are friendly.
	II	16	Loving care. To grow more loving everyday.
		17	He loved the youngest daughter.
		19	He was very kind to her.
		24	How friendly you are.
		59	No one cared for him.
		67	Care.
	III	68	Fell in love with the beautiful girl.
		72	Hurt no living thing.
Telugu	I	5	నేను నా దేశమును ప్రేమించుచున్నాను.
	II	9	అమ్మ బుజ్జగించి మెల్లగ చెప్పును.
		11	బుజ్జగించి
		15	...... మొక్కలను పెంచవలెను.
		32	....ప్రీతితో. ....ప్రేమకొలది.

Subject & Class		*Page no.*	*Related content in form of terms/words/ meanings/situations*
		50	కూర్మితో చదివించారు.
		51	ప్రేమ. కూర్మి.
	III	28	చెలిమి.
		32	.... దేవుని ప్రేమించుట.
		33	....ప్రేమ.
		41	తన బిడ్డలను ప్రేమతో చూచి.....
		56	ప్రేమ ......
Hindi R	II	27	... ... आदर किजिए ।
Hindi B	III	22	... ... बहुत प्यारा है ।
		29	सब उसको प्यार करते थे ... ...
		55	माता-पिता की प्यार भरी गोद में ... ...
		58	... ... प्यारे बच्चों ... ...
Soc. Std.	I	7	They love one another.
		17	To be kind to animals.
		37	We should be polite to each other.
		38	We must be kind to our classmates.
	II	55	Love-playing with your pets and toys.
		56	Children make friends at play.
	III	45	Do not quarrel or fight with each other.
		59	Kings must care for the welfare of their people.
Science	I	30	Be kind to animals. When animals fall ill, we must show them to a doctor.
		39	Do not pull the plant.
	II	13	Living beings need care and attention.
		22	Look after pets with love and affection.

(where R denotes Hindi Rachana)

The content shown in table 5.2 relates to 'affection and friendliness'. When the teacher comes across the content she has to incorporate the suggested activities for the development of the behavioural trait. For example, when the teacher is dealing with Class I English, the content on pages 54 i.e., "Monkeys were friendly with the squirrel" and 57 i.e., "Be polite. You are friendly", she can adopt the activity of taking the children to an excursion. In another instance, with children of Class II, while teaching English content on page no.19, "He was very kind to her", the teacher can follow the role-play which enables them to feel that living things should not be harmed. The activities are described below:

1. Students are divided into two groups – A and B. In the role-play, the students of group B, are asked to scratch the back and move a rubber lizard on the hands of group A members. The students feel the pinch and shout. At this juncture, the teacher poses a question as to what a tree feels when a squirrel runs up the trunk and when it is cut. Students of group A, having felt a strange feeling, answer that, the trees feel the scratching and hurt.

   Next time, the roles of groups A and B are reversed.

Thus, the students understand and internalise that the plants and animals are living things like human beings and should not be harmed. This activity develops affection towards other living things.

2. The students are taken on an excursion – a visit to zoo, a visit to a park, a visit to a planetarium, a field trip to a picnic spot, a field trip to biscuit factory, etc. On their journey, the students interact with each other, such as knowing their names, likes and dislikes, place of residence, names of their friends & siblings, and so on.

This activity develops 'friendliness' in the students because their interaction enables them to come closer and develops affinity towards each other.

Alertness

The content for 'alertness' found in the text-books is shown in the table 5.3.

Table 5.3. Content Analysis for 'Alertness'

Subject & Class		*Page no.*	*Related content in form of terms/words/ meanings/situations*
English	I	53	Rama stood watching.
	II	84	Columbus sat watching them.
		88	Carefully watching.
	III	9	Watch dogs went around the Ark to see if all was safe.
		15	Goldlilocks awoke in a fright.
		19	"Wake", said the sunshine. "Wake" said the voice.
		37	Watching ships
Telugu	I	79	జాగరూకుఁడగుము.
	II	15	చాల జాగ్రత్తగ ... ...
		26	ఆవులు కాసే ... ...
	III	11	... చాల జాగ్రత్తగ పోనిత్తురు.
		49	... కావలసిన కట్టుబాట్లు చేసికొనిరి.
		64	[illegible]
Hindi R	I	18	समझ
	III	31	समझदार
Soc. Std.	I	15	They are watching the animals.
	II	38	Before crossing the road, we should look to our left and to our right.
		39	Be careful on roads.
		51	The watchman guards our houses.
Science	I	40	Children watch plants grow.
	II	14	Protect the crop from grazing animals.
		56	Plant a seed and watch it grow.

The content of the table 5.3 relates to the behavioural trait 'alertness'. The following activities are suggested to be incorporated by the teacher when she comes across the related content to develop 'alertness' in their students. For example, the content on page 84 i.e. "Columbus sat watching them" for Class II English, provides ample scope for the teacher to incorporate the activity describing and predicting the weather conditions. Similarly, for the content of Social Studies Class II on page 38, i.e. "Before crossing the road, we should look to our left and to our right", the teacher is suggested to adopt the role-play enabling the students to observe traffic rules. The activities are as follows:

1. Let the students discuss the weather. How many types of weather conditions can they describe? Ask the students to prepare symbolic drawings of different weather conditions like the ones shown below in the figure 5.1.

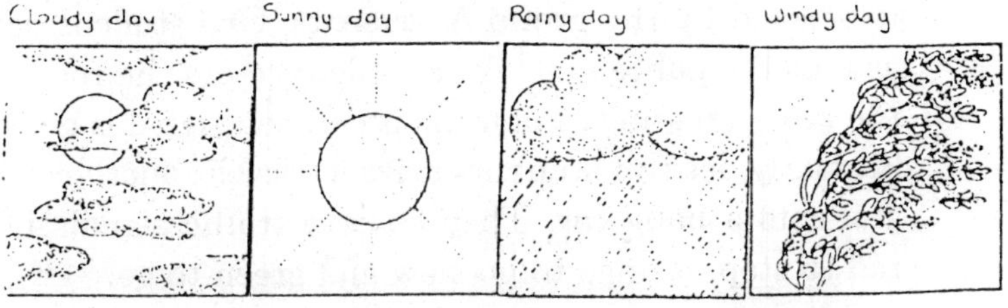

Figure 5.1: Symbolic Drawings of different Weather Conditions.

The students can develop symbols according to the climate in their area.

Students should make a chart with a square of 4 cm x 4 cm for each day of the month. They should be asked to fill each of these squares with a symbolic drawing appropriate to the weather prevailing on that day. For example, if the season is monsoon and it is very cloudy on Monday the 1st, the students will stick the "Very cloudy" grey-coloured symbol on the square. On Tuesday the 2nd, if it is rainy, the students will paste the "Rainy Day" black-coloured umbrella symbol on the square and so on.

Ask the students to make weather predictions each morning as they come to school and to record them. Were they right? If so how many times each month? They could record right or wrong predictions by putting a "v" or "x' in each corner of the day's square alongwith the correct symbol.

Later, ask the students to compare their observations with the weather forecasts in the newspaper brought to the classroom by the teacher or on radio or television at home. (Joy of Learning, Handbook of Environmental Education Activities, 1986).

2. Students are made into groups of nine each. Let the school premises be prepared as a traffic system with cross-roads having zebra crossings for pedestrians, signals for pedestrians as well as motorists. A role-play is enacted by the group A students. One student acts as a traffic policeman. Four students cross the road on the zebra crossings when the pedestrian signal is green. Similarly, let two students drive a tricycle, another two students a baby car. They observe traffic signals i.e., red to stop, orange to go slow and green to go.

Traffic signals are used to demonstrate that it is dangerous to cross the road when it is red.

3. A group of 10 students plays a game of musical chairs. The students go around the 9 chairs arranged in a circle. They stop and sit on the chairs when the music stops. As there are only 9 chairs, only 9 students will sit on the chairs and the tenth student who is not able to secure a seat is viewed as not attentive. Likewise, the game is played upto the last chair and the winner is rewarded.

This activity of musical chairs develops alertness in the students because they are always on the watch.

Altruism

The content for 'altruism' found in the text-books is represented below in the table 5.4.

Table 5.4. Content Analysis for 'Altruism'

Subject & Class			*Page no.*	*Related content in form of terms/words/ meanings/situations*
English		I	57	If you are selfish, you will not have friends.
			80	Thinking only of yourself.
		II	46	We want all the water.
Telugu		II	56	... మెలమెచ్చుల దాతయతడు .....
		III	63	ఉపకారికి ... ...
Hindi	B	III	17	भलाई के लिये हमें त्याग करना चाहिये ।
			54	... लालच बुरी बला है ।
	R	III	13	सदा त्याग करो ।

The content reported in the table 5.4 is related to the behavioural trait 'altruism'. When the teacher is teaching the content related to 'altruism', she may incorporate the activities suggested by the investigator for the development of 'altruism'. For example, the teacher can incorporate the first activity i.e. rearing a pup or some other domestic animal, while teaching the content on page 57 i.e. "If you are selfish, you will not have friends". Similarly, the second activity for the aspect of 'principle of considering the well-being of others first' can be incorporated at the time of teaching the content on page 80 i.e. "Thinking only of yourself" of Class I English. The activities are shown below:

1. A two-week old pup is given to each of the two groups of students. They nurture the pups with the food they bring to school.

After three months, the nurturing of the two pups is evaluated and the class which reared the pup to a healthy one is reinforced.

The healthy pup received more attention, care and food, because of unselfishness of the students.

Further, the reinforcement of one class by the teacher enables the students of the other group to review their behaviour and try to be unselfish in future.

'The principle of considering the well-being and happiness of others first' can be developed in the following manner:

2. During a potluck lunch session, the teacher asks the children to give foodstuffs, first to the neighbours and then feed themselves. In simple terms "Athidhi Devo Bavah".

This activity is repeated for the children to internalise the aspect of 'considering the well-being and happiness of others first'.

Co-operation

The content for 'co-operation' is represented in the table 5.5.

Table 5.5. Content Analysis for 'Co-operation'

Subject & Class		*Page no.*	*Related content in form of terms/words/ meanings/situations*
Telugu	II	19	అందరము కలిసి.... ...
		20	అందరము కలిసి మెలిసి ఉండవలెను.
		22	కట్టెలు మోపుగ కలిసి ఉన్నందున ... ...
	III	47	కృతఘ్నత చేసినవారికి సాయము చేయుట కూడదు.
Hindi B	III	29	वह सबकी सहायता करता था ।
		57	मिलाकर देश बनाओ ।
		58	मिलाकर देश बनाओ ।
R	III	27	रंग सात में ... ...
Soc. Std.	I	7	They live together in the same house.

	III	35	Men live in societies and they have needs common to all. These needs are called collective needs.
		41	People must co-operate with these institutions to get good service from them.
Maths	I	22	One more boy comes and joins them.
		27	How many birds are there altogether?
		28	How many books are there altogether?
		73	We join equivalent sets in multiplication.
	II	53	Add together 9 and 5.
		87	How many students are there altogether?
		91	While multiplying three numbers we may multiply them in any order. The product remains the same. It is called associative law.
	III	15	Find the total population of the hamlets put together.
		44	How much money have they together?
		45	What is the total population of these two schools together?
		113	The following pairs are equivalent fractions.

(where Maths – Mathematics)

The content in the table 5.5 is related to 'co-operation'. It is suggested that the teacher should include the following activities to develop 'co-operation' in the students as and when she comes across this content. For example, while teaching the content on page 41 i.e. "People must co-operate with these institutions to get good service from them", of social studies the teacher can adopt the first activity, i.e., the one which enables them to be responsible for the material. The details are given below:

1. Let each student be the incharge of relevant pictures and resources, posters, useful equipment such as magnifying lenses, plaster of paris or dough, pencils, paper, scissors, etc. Each child is responsible to give the material and keep safe after its use. Each student when he is to use the material borrows from another

student, i.e., if a student is using red pencil, the other student has to use blue pencil. Likewise, when one student cuts paper by using scissors, let that be pasted in a scrap book by another student.

The teacher observes that students use the material one after another and complete the work assigned to each of them.

2. The students feel fun to have a small garden of their own. They can grow radishes, greentail onions, lettuce and pumpkins. Let one student get the seeds, another child sow them, still another water them. The students will be proud of themselves and would check their plants many times a day. In this activity students work together and it is inferred in a general manner to develop 'co-operation'.

Co-ordination

The content for 'co-ordination' found in the text-books is represented in the table 5.6.

Table 5.6. Content Analysis for 'Co-ordination'

Subject & Class		*Page no.*	*Related content in form of terms/words/ meanings/situations*
Hindi B	I	28	लोग किसको ढकेल रहे हैं ।
Hindi R	I	28	मिलना
Soc. Std.	I	32	We play together in school.
	III	45	The Government appoints men to do some jobs for the people.
		48	List the names of officers at block level.
Maths	III	41	Numbers can be added in any order.
		61	Students are arranged in three rows.
Science	II	16	Lions move in groups in the forests.
		56	Children can learn to put up a fence with pieces of bamboo or cane.

The content in the table 5.6 is related to 'co-ordination'. While teaching the content related to co-ordination the teacher is suggested to incorporate the following activity for the development of 'co-ordination' in the students. For instance, the teacher can adopt this activity for the content given on page 45 "the Government appoints men to do some jobs for the people" of Class III Social studies where the students learn the importance of cause to function together or in proper order. The activity is:

Let ten students hold placards with a sentence each of a known story. Ask the students to jumble up. The audience (the remaining students) try to build story in a sequence.

When a student from the audience identifies and reads the first sentence, the student holding the first sentence comes and stands in front of the teacher. Then, another student from the audience spells out the second sentence to make a meaningful story, the student holding the second sentence comes and stands to the left of the first student. Likewise, as students complete the story, one student after another comes in order and stands one besides the other. This exercise develops a sense of 'cause to function in proper order' in the student.

This activity meant for the students of Class III, develops 'co-ordination'.

This activity can be repeated with different groups of students with a different story, if the strength of the class is more than ten.

The same activity can be repeated for Class II students with words forming a proverb/saying/idiom/phrase, etc. and Class I students with letters forming a word.

Courage

The content for 'courage' found in the text-books is shown in the table 5.7.

Table 5.7: Analysis of Content for the Behavioural Trait 'Courage'

Subject & Class		*Page no.*	*Related content in form of terms/words/ meanings/situations*
English	I	23	They had to obey the king's order.
	II	19	She would go and live with the beast.
		29	They can work with a will.
		45	Smaller animals were not afraid of the big fierce animals.
		47	We too can frighten them.
		62	Being bold.
		78	Brave.
	III	9	He stuck his blunt nose into the hole.
Telugu	I	39	ఆ రైతు పౌరుషము చూడుము.
	II	12	శౌర్యము తలచండి. వీరులైన విజయము గాంచండి.
		13	శౌర్యము.
		39	... బాధలను నిబ్బరముగ అనుభవించెను.
		42	బెదురు లేకుండ.
	III	5	నగధర శౌరి.
		6	ధైర్యమే లక్ష్మి
		7	... ధైర్యముగ నుండవలెను. ధైర్యము .....
Hindi R	I	29	धीरज
Hindi B	III	40	रानी लक्ष्मीबाई बहुत बहादुर थी ।

The content given in the table 5.7 is related to the behavioural trait 'courage'. When the teacher comes across this content, she can incorporate the following suggested activities to develop 'courage' in the students. For example, the aspect of 'boldness' can be developed through the first activity at the time of teaching content on page 29 i.e. "They can work with a will" of Class II of English. Likewise, the content on page 9 i.e. "He stuck his blunt nose into the hole" of Class III English provides scope for the teacher to incorporate the second activity involving competitions. The details are as follows:

1. In a general manner, the teacher reinforces the student who speaks the truth. This develops 'boldness' in the students as their behaviour is recognised by the teacher and in front of others.

2. Students of Class III are made into groups of 5. One student from Class IV is selected and is asked to lose the race deliberately when he/she is competing in a running race alongwith one group from Class III. At the end of the competition one student of Class III wins. Thus, confidence of the student is reinforced.

The activity is repeated with another student from Class IV with the same instructions and conduct competition alongwith another group of Class III. Likewise, another student from Class III wins and develops 'braveness'.

Decision Making Ability

The content for decision-making ability found in the text-books is shown in the table 5.8.

Table 5.8: Content Analysis for 'Decision-making Ability"

Subject & Class		*Page no.*	*Related content in form of terms/words/ meanings/situations*
English	I	65	The king decided to test his cleverness.
	II	45	They finally decided to go in search of water.
		51	He decided to find a treasure.
		61	Jay decided to go home.
		78	Decide whether they end in 't' or 'd'.
		83	Columbus decided to leave Spain.
		88	To make up one's mind
	III	40	When strange birds settled on the masts of the ships, Columbus knew that land must be near.

		48	An idea struck her.
		74	Amazed to see your wisdom in the court.
		75	Your Majesty, shall solve this problem.
		84	Having good judgement.
Telugu	I	64	చెప్పుకో చూతాము
		65	పొడుపు కథలు
	II	6	.... తగవులను విచారణ చేయుచుండెను.
		8	తీర్పు. విచారణ.
		21	.... కట్టెల మోపు విలువలేక పోయెను.
		22	నిశ్చయము. కాబట్టి కలిసియుండిన మా జాతికి ఎవరును రాలేరు.
	III	50	.... పండ్లు నాటి కందునట్లు చేసికొన కోరెను. ... బుద్ధిహీనత అని గ్రహించుకొనెను.
		56	...... దొంగతనము చేయకూడదని అతడు నిశ్చయించుకొనెను.
Hindi B	III	36	मैं ने निश्चय किया कि ... ...
		41	दृढ
		43	... ... उसे युकित सूझी ।
		54	... ... पूरे सवाल हल हो जायेंगे ।
Science	II	14	Insects and fungus attack plants causing many diseases. Insecticides and fungicides must be sprayed.

The contents of the table 5.8 is related to 'decision making ability'. The teacher can incorporate the following activities to develop the ability in the students as and when she comes across their content. For instance, the activity involving maze problems developing 'judging' aspect can be included at the time of teaching content on page 14 i.e. "Insects and fungus attack plants causing many diseases. Insecticides and fungicides must be sprayed" of Class II Science. In the same manner, the activity of finding the hidden toys enabling the students to develop 'an ability to decide and act accordingly' can be incorporated while dealing with the content on page 45 i.e. "They finally decided to go in search of water" of Class II English. The details are:

1. A maze problem consisting of a rabbit and a carrot is given to a student. He is asked to find the path for the rabbit to reach the carrot. The student after few trials succeeds in the task.

In this activity, the student considers different paths, of which only one is a correct one, thus developing the 'judging' ability.

2. The students are made into two groups, A and B, of 5 each. Let group A have 5 toys and decide with respect to its hiding place. Group A students give clues regarding the hiding place to group B to find out the toys. Group B finds out the toys with the help of clues given to them. The teacher encourages the students to hide the toys in various different places.

This activity enables the students to 'decide and act accordingly'. The students of the group A decide about the hiding place for toys whereas the group B students decide about locating the toys.

The exercise is then repeated with the roles exchanged. Let group B decide the hiding place for toys and group A find them.

This activity covers ten students at a time. If the strength of the class is more, the activity is repeated.

Enthusiasm

Content for 'enthusiasm' is represented in the table 5.9.

Table 5.9: Content Analysis for 'Enthusiasm'

Subject & Class		*Page no.*	*Related content in form of terms/words/ meanings/situations*
English	I	80	Strong desire.
	II	17	Fond of pets.
		24	Interesting.

The content related to the behavioural trait 'enthusiasm' is reported in the table 5.9. When the teacher is teaching this content, she is suggested to incorporate the following activities for developing enthusiasm. For example, the 'strong feeling of admiration or interest' – an aspect of enthusiasm which develops through an activity of collecting the material, at the time of dealing with the content on page 17 i.e. "Fond of pets" of Class II English. The activities are given below:

1. Students are made into groups of 5 each. Each group is asked to collect as many stones as possible and bring with them the following day. The teacher collects the coloured stones from the groups and makes a note of it.

This activity can be repeated by telling them to improve the performance further. Likewise, the students try to improve their performance which the teacher reinforces verbally and develops enthusiasm in them.

2. The students are taken to a part where different types of trees are present. Divide the class into groups of four or five and let them settle down in different places. Let the students observe a few trees and recognise the main parts of a tree. Let them practice drawing or sketching the main parts of a tree.

The students can be asked to sketch the shapes of the trees highlighting the positions of the different parts and paste them in a scrap book.

Independent Thinking

The content for 'independent thinking' found in the text-books is given in the table 5.10

The table 5.10 shows the content related to 'independent thinking'. The teacher is suggested to incorporate the following activities as and when she comes across this content and develops 'independent thinking'. For instance, while dealing with the content on i.e. "स्वयं" of Class

Table 5.10: Content Analysis for 'Independent Thinking'

Subject & Class			*Page no.*	*Related content in form of terms/words/ meanings/situations*
Hindi	B	III	38	स्वयं
			57	आजादी ... ...
			58	आजादी ... ...
Hindi	R	III	25	स्वतंत्र

III Hindi, the teacher can incorporate this activity of developing pictures over the lines. The activities are as follows:

1. Students are given pieces of paper on which there are lines such as ---, |, L, /, \, V. The teacher asks thom to develop pictures over these lines in ten minutes. At the end of the session, the teacher collects the papers and finds many number of pictures. The teacher reinforces the students' efforts.

In this activity, students are neither under the compulsion of the teacher nor taking any guidance from the teacher, but are thinking independently to draw pictures. Thus, they develop 'independent thinking'.

2. Students are made into five groups. The first student in each group is given a separate story comprising of four or five sentences and is asked to give a title to it. Student who give an appropriate title to the story is reinforced by the teacher.

The activity is repeated with the second, third, fourth, and fifth set of students with different stories on different sessions.

This activity develops 'independent thinking' in students because they do not take anybody's help in giving a title to the story.

Initiative

The content for 'initiative' found in the text-books is shown in the table 5.11.

Table 5.11. Analysis of Content for 'Initiative'

Subject & Class		*Page no.*	*Related content in form of terms/words/ meanings/situations*
English	II	11	Alice's first adventure in wonderland.
	III	40	He discovered new islands.
Telugu	II	7	...అతనికి ఒక ఉపాయము తోచినది.

The content shown in table 5.11 is related to 'initiative'. The teacher is suggested to include the following activities when she is teaching this content to develop 'initiative'. For example, the activity related to the aspect of 'an ability to act without being prompted by others' can be incorporated at the content of page 11 i.e. "Alice's first adventure in wonderland" of Class II English. Similarly, the other activity involving a problem situation can be adopted at the time of teaching content on page 40 i.e. "He discovered new islands" of Class III English. The details are given below:

1. The students are shown a different drawing or painting technique, at least once a week. How the medium works- with water and without water, on different papers, to make a misty picture, a watery picture and so on is demonstrated. Students follow what the teacher does and in addition have an opportunity to explore the media for themselves. They often have their own ideas for techniques.

The students are encouraged and helped to display pieces of their own work or models in an interesting and aesthetic way on a display board. They learn to mount two dimensional works with borders and place models on their own display mats. Appropriate labels are added later.

In this activity the students 'act without being prompted by others' as demonstrated in the work of their display.

2. Students were divided into groups of 5 each. To the Group A, the teacher shows a series of pictures related to a 'thirsty crow' as given below in the figure 5.2.

Figure 5.2: Pictures related to the 'Thirsty crow'.

The students are asked to describe the pictures. According to them, the 1st picture shows – a crow was very thirsty; 2nd picture – it wandered here and there for water and at last saw a water pot near a well; 3rd picture – it looked inside the pot. There was very little water in the pot; 4th picture –It saw some stones near the well.

The students are asked the manner in which the crow quenches its thirst. After analysing the situation, one student replies that the crow picks up some stones, puts them one by one into the pot, the water level comes up and the crow drinks water.

This activity enables the student 'to see what needs to be done & enterprise enough to do it'.

The activity is repeated for other students and also with different problem situations.

Leadership

The following table 5.12 shows the content analysis for the behavioural trait 'leadership'.

Table 5.12: Analysis of Content for the Behavioural Trait 'Leadership'

Subject & Class		*Page no.*	*Related content in form of terms/words/ meanings/situations*
English	II	59	The monkey asked him to follow him.
Hindi B	III	57	आगे बढते जाओ ।
		58	आगे बढते जाओ ।
Soc. Std.	III	53	They first invented fire to burn the meat to eat.
		65	He secured many followers in Madina.

The content in the table 5.12 is related to 'leadership'. As and when the teacher is teaching this content and would like to develop 'leadership' in the students, she is suggested to include the following activity. For example, the teacher can incorporate the activity at the time of teaching the content of page 59 i.e., "The monkey asked him to follow him" of Class I English. The details are given below:

Let the students be divided into groups of 3 each. The teacher takes the students of the first group and asks them to stand in a line – one behind the other. The teacher stands in front of the first group and asks the students to hold the dress of the student in front so as to form a link.

The teacher demonstrates the game of a train wherein he/she is the engine and the students behind act as compartments and go around and inside the classroom alongwith the teacher.

After a few minutes the teacher leaves the first group alone, and asks the students of all the groups including the first group to stand one behind the other. The teacher asks the students who are in the front in each group to act as an engine and the others follow them around and inside the classroom.

Later, the teacher asks the students to exchange their roles so as to see that each student in a group to get an opportunity to lead the members.

Rationality

The content for 'rationality' is given in the table 5.13.

Table 5.13: Content Analysis for 'Rationality'

Subject & Class		*Page no.*	*Related content in form of terms/words/ meanings/situations*
Hindi B	III	42	... पानी ऊपर आगया और ... ...
Science	III	20	What made this to rotate?
		21	Why does water go into the tumbler?

The content in the table 5.13 is related to 'rationality. The teacher can incorporate the following activities as and when she comes across this content and would like to develop 'rationality'. For instance, at the time of teaching content related to page 21 i.e., "Why does water go into the tumbler?" of Class III Science, the teacher can incorporate the first activity involving working principle of see-saw play object. The details are given below:

1. Let groups of two students play a see-saw one on each side. Another student joins them and sits on one side. Then the opposite side which has one student goes up. Ask them why it happens so.

The student gives reason as to why it goes up. The side which has one student goes up because the weight on that side is less than the opposite side which has two students. Thus, explaining the phenomenon in a rational manner depicts rationality.

2. Let the students play 'tug of war game' – three versus five. The group which has five students wins the game.

The students are asked why the group of five students won the game. They give reason that the group of five which is larger than a group of three, has more strength and so it won.

Realism

The analysis of content for 'realism' found in the text-books is shown in the table 5.14.

Table 5.14: Content Analysis for 'Realism'

Subject & Class		*Page no.*	*Related content in form of terms/words/ meanings/situations*
English	I	40	King looked across the garden and saw a poor old beggar. "What a bad day," he thought.

The content in the table 5.14 is related to 'realism'. The teacher is suggested to incorporate the following activities for developing 'realism' in the students when she is teaching this content. For example, the suggested activity can be included at the time of content related to page 40 i.e., King looked across the garden and saw a poor old beggar. "What a bad day," he thought, of Class I English. The details are as follows:

The students are given the mutilated toys, say, a duck with a broken limb, a car with two wheels, etc. alongwith clay. They are asked to prepare models.

Even before they replicate the toys, students try to mend the mutilated toys to make it a whole. Then, the students prepare exactly the same type of clay models as they see from the given mutilated toys.

The students who replicate the model as given in the mutilated toys have developed 'realism' because they are practical with regard to the thing or situation that is described or the representation of familiar things as they really are.

Sharing

The analysis of content for 'sharing' found in the text-books is represented in the table 5.15.

Table 5.15: Content Analysis for 'Sharing'

Subject & Class		*Page no.*	*Related content in form of terms/words/ meanings/situations*
English	I	57	You must be willing to share what you have with your friends.
Hindi B	I	24	का का ख साथी ।
Maths	II	97	60 mangoes are distributed among 8 boys.
		101	Share 8 apples between 4 girls.
		102	Mary distributed 333 chocolates to her friends on her birthday.

The content shown in the table 5.15 is related to 'sharing'. The teacher can incorporate the following activities when she is teaching this content and would like to develop 'sharing'. For instance, the suggested activity of sharing during the lunch session can be incorporated when the teacher is dealing with the content of page 57 i.e., "You must be willing to share what you have with your friends" of Class I English. The details are given below:

1. Everybody during the lunch session, let the students have a common sharing lunch. Each student gives a portion of his foodstuff to others, who in turn give portion of their's to still others.

The teacher reinforces the appropriate behaviour by involving themselves in the activity.

In this activity there is 'giving away a part of what a person possesses' – an aspect of sharing.

2. During the occasions of school functions, national and religious festivals, let the students be made into groups of five each. Then, they are allotted the work of keeping the classroom surroundings clean and green. Group A members are asked to pick up small stones, bits of paper and other unwanted material from inside and outside the classroom. Group B members hold the broomstick and sweep the floor for cleaning. Next, Group C members cut the colour papers, make different shapes from coloured paper and decorate the classroom.

Likewise, this activity can be conducted for 15 students at a time. If the strength of the class is more than 15, then the activity is repeated with other students on a different occasion.

This activity provides them to 'endure jointly the hardships and fruits of the work' turned out by the students. Thus, endurance in 'sharing' with others is developed in the students.

Sportsmanship

The analysis of content for 'Sportsmanship' is shown below in the table 5.16.

Table 5.16: Analysis of Content for 'Sportsmanship'

Subject & Class		*Page no.*	*Related content in form of terms/words/ meanings/situations*
Telugu	II	19	...వచ్చిన ఆట ఆడుదము.
Soc. Std.	I	15	We play games in school and at home.
		33	There is a playground to play games.
	II	27	The games-teacher teach us how to play games.
		56	We see children playing in a park.
Maths	II	87	If two teams play the kabaddi game, how many players do they have? There are seven teams of koko participating during Independence day celebration.

The table 5.16 shows the content related to 'sportsmanship'. The teacher can incorporate the following suggested activities while teaching this content. For example, the activity suggested by the investigator can be incorporated at the time of teaching the content on page 27 i.e., "The games-teacher teach us how to play games" of Class II Social studies. The details are as follows:

In a simulated condition five tasks of increasing difficulty are presented to the students. Say, a student is able to do all the tasks successfully, another student completes 4 tasks, still another 3 tasks, and so on and so forth.

The teacher reinforces the students who performed 3 tasks successfully and develops in them the urge to perform all the 5 tasks in the next session. Similarly, a student who performed all the tasks successfully interacts with a student who is able to do 3 tasks and builds confidence in him.

Likewise, the teacher reinforcement and the successful students interaction with the students of lesser performance will improve the latter's performance in the next session.

In this activity, the successful students look upon and interact with the less performed and also the latter develop tolerance and strive hard to succeed.

Thus, the aspect of 'willing to take risks and is not down-heartened, if lost', is developed in students.

Sympathy

The analysis of content for 'sympathy' found in the text-books is shown in the table 5.17.

The table 5.17 shows the content related to 'sympathy'. When the teacher is teaching this content, she can incorporate the following suggested activity to develop the behavioural trait 'sympathy' in the students. For instance,

Table 5.17: Content Analysis for 'Sympathy'

Subject & Class			*Page no.*	*Related content in form of terms/words/ meanings/situations*
Telugu		I	35	దేవుని దయ
		II	41	... శ్రీరామునకు దయ కలిగెను. ... దయకలిగిన...
			42	శ్రీరామునికి తనపై దయ కలిగినదని గ్రహించెను.
		III	33	... దయాగుణము ... ...
			41	... ఆమె మీద దయ కలుగలేదు.
			64	దయ చూపుంటే
Hindi	B	III	30	... से यह सब नहीं देखा गया ।

the suggested activity can be incorporated by the teacher while teaching the content i.e., "राजू से यह सब नहीं देखा गया" of Class III Hindi Bal Saritha.

Let students form pairs. One in each pair is blind-folded and each pair is asked to walk through a series of obstacles like a ditch, tree or an overhanging branch with the partner who can see, leading. If obstacles are not available, these can be created with marks on the ground, posting volunteers to be trees, or using furniture (Joy of Learning, Handbook of Environmental Education Activities, 1986).

The partner who leads should do so without talking, by taking the hand of his blind-folded partner and makes him feel the obstacles and difficulties the blind face in the daily life situations. This develops sympathetic feeling in the students.

After a while, the roles in each pair should be reversed.

This activity can be conducted for ten students. If the strength is more, the activity is repeated a number of times on different days.

This activity of leading the blind develops 'sympathy' in the students.

From the above discussion, it could be seen that 'hypothess no. 4, the classroom activities to develop essential behavioural traits to meet disasters can be fused into the existing primary school curriculum" has been realised. Thus, the objective no.4 'to incorporate the developed activities in the existing primary school curriculum' is achieved.

The details of the content analysis for all the behavioural traits so far discussed is shown in a consolidated form in the table 5.18.

Spontaneity

It is evident from the table 5.18 that the existing curricular content is friendly for the seventeen behavioural traits except for 'spontaneity' and the suggested activities could be accommodated. Hence, it is suggested that the proposed activity for 'spontaneity' the teachers should organise specifically and specially the activities that are described, at least for three to four times during the academic year. The details are given below:

1. Letters of the alphabet are written separately on small pieces of paper, rolled and placed in a small jar. The teacher asks the students to pick up a paper, spell out as many words starting with that alphabet, as he can in one minute. The teacher notes down the words of the student. Similarly, another student picks up another alphabet and spells out words and the teacher makes a note of it. Likewise ten students are asked to continue with the activity. At the end of the activity, the teacher reinforces the students by repeating their words and the student who spelt maximum words is given a small gift (a pencil, an eraser, a crayon, a book, etc.).

If the students are many in number, then the activity is repeated in another session with other students.

Table 5.18: Content Analysis of the Text-books for the Behavioural Traits

	Behavioural trait *Class 3*		*Subject*	*Class 1*	*Class 2*
1.	Adjustment				
		Hindi			'B 44
		Soc Std.	24	23, 24, 49,	50
		Science	30	40	13, 15
2.	Affection & Friendliness				
		English	54, 57	16, 17, 19, 24, 59, 67	68, 72
		Telugu	5	9, 11, 15, 32, 50, 51	28, 32, 33, 41, 56
		Hindi		R27	B22, 29, 55, 58
		Soc. Std.	7, 17, 37, 38	55, 56	45, 59
		Science	30, 39	13, 22	
3.	Alertness				
		English	53	84, 88	9, 15, 19, 37
		Telugu	79	15, 26	11, 49, 64
		Hindi	R18		R31
		Soc. Std.	15	38, 39, 51	
		Science	40	14, 56	
4.	Altruism				
		English	57, 80	46	
		Telugu		56	63
		Hindi			B17, 54, R13

(where B is Hindi Bal Saritha; R is Hindi Rachana; Soc. Std. Is Social Studies; Maths is Mathematics; numbers denote the page numbers in the text-books)

5.	Co-operation				
		Telugu		19, 20, 22	47
		Hindi			B29, 57, 58, R27
		Soc. Std.	7		35, 41
		Maths	22, 27, 28, 73	53, 87, 91	15, 44, 45, 113
6.	Co-ordination				
		Hindi	B28, R28		
		Soc. Std.	32		45, 48
		Maths			41, 61
		Science		16, 56	
7.	Courage				
		English	23	19, 29, 45, 47, 62, 78	9
		Telugu	39	12, 13, 39, 42	5, 6, 7
		Hindi	R29		B40
8.	Decision-making ability				
		English	65	45, 51, 61, 78, 83, 88	40, 48, 74, 75, 84
		Telugu	64, 65	6, 8, 21, 22	50, 56
		Hindi			B36, 41, 43, 54
		Science		14	
9.	Enthusiasm				
		English	80	17, 24	
10.	Independent thinking				
		Hindi			B38, 57, 58, R25
11.	Initiative				
		English		11	40
		Telugu		7	

12.	Leadership				
		English	59		
		Hindi			B57, 58
		Soc. Std.			53, 65
13.	Rationality				
		Hindi			B42
		Science			20, 21
14.	Realism				
		English	40		
15.	Sharing				
		Maths		97, 101, 102	
		English	57		
		Hindi	B24		
16.	Sportsmanship				
		Telugu		19	
		Soc. Std.	15, 33	27, 56	
		Maths		87	
17	Sympathy				
		Telugu	35	41, 42	33, 41, 64
		Hindi			B30

In this activity, students are responding naturally on the spot and trying to give maximum number of words in the prescribed time limit. Thus, 'spontaneity' will be developed in them.

2. Plaster of paris, dough, clay and other moulding material is placed in the classroom. Each student is asked to prepare as many number of objects as possible of his choice in fifteen minutes from the given material.

At the end of fifteen minutes, students prepare objects such as a stick, a plate, a ball, a rat, a bat, and so on from different materials. The teacher reinforces the student's efforts in preparing the objects and the student who prepared the maximum number of objects is given a small gift (a pencil, a scale, a crayon, a book, etc.,).

As the students respond spontaneously to prepare maximum number of objects from the given moulding materials in the prescribed time limit, they develop 'spontaneity' behaviour.

Conclusions

The first objective – "to list out the disasters that occur in India with a natural trigger", as tested through hypothesis no. 1, i.e., "there are certain natural disasters which recur regularly in India", has been realised.

The second objective, i.e., "to establish behaviour traits essential to meet natural disaster situations", is tested through hypothesis no. 2 – "certain behavioural traits to meet disaster situations can be developed through classroom activities at the primary school level", has been realised.

The third objective – "to suggest the curricular activities at primary school level for developing the behavioural traits essential to meet the disaster situations", as tested through hypothesis no. 3. i.e., "the essential behavioural traits to meet disaster situations can be developed through classroom activities at the primary school level," has been realized.

The fourth objective – "to incorporate the developed activities in the existing primary school curriculum", is tested through hypothesis no. 4 i.e., "the classroom activities to develop essential behavioural traits to meet disasters can be fused into the existing primary school curriculum", has been realised.

Thus, the present study concludes that:

1. Natural disasters recur regularly in India.
2. The behavioural traits essential to meet the disaster situations are – adjustment, affection & friendliness, alertness, altruism, co-operation, co-ordination, courage, decision-making ability, enthusiasm, independent thinking, initiative, leadership, rationality, realism, sharing, spontaneity, sportsmanship and sympathy.
3. The essential behavioural traits to meet disaster situations can be developed through classroom activities at the primary school level.
4. The classroom activities to develop essential behavioural traits to meet disasters can be incorporated into the existing primary school curriculum.

A Sincere Confession

1. Ability to face situations like a disaster depends on the total personality of an individual. As it is very difficult and rather impractical to define personality and to address the question of improving personality, a set of behavioural traits has been adopted to describe the essential characteristics which enables the individual in particular and the society in general to face disaster situations. Therefore, it is natural that the list of behavioural traits listed as essential in the present study is not exhaustive.
2. Similarly, the activities planned by the investigator have been developed based on the perceptions of the

researchers and through a review of literature like publications of International Decade for Natural Disaster Reduction, etc. It is therefore, to be stressed that the list of activities is not exhaustive but only illustrative. The activities may be modified and adopted according to local conditions. The investigator would consider his work be immensely successful, if it can inspire researchers/educationists to develop other activities to inculcate the essential behavioural traits.

3. The evaluation of the performance of the children for confirming the development of the expected behaviour also has to be rigorously thought over and different types of activities have to be developed for confirming the existence of the expected behaviour in the children.

4. The activities planned to have been adopted with a view to incorporate them in the existing curriculum of the schools of Andhra Pradesh. As such they are not totally devoid of culture specificity. Researchers from other parts of India and abroad may kindly exercise due care to see that suitable modifications are made to suit their respective cultures.

Further Suggestions

1. The time schedule was restricted and inspite of working for more than five years, the longitudinal character has not been thoroughly reflected. Therefore, it is suggested that some National Agency should take over this problem for a longitudinal study and prescribe a new pattern for Universal Elementary Education by incorporating that activities that are revealed as useful through the present study.

2. Activities suggested to be included in the curriculum are arrived after dozens of brain-storming sessions conducted by the supervisor alongwith other research scholars which, of course, are still not comprehensive.

Hence, it will be in the fitness of suggestions to say that these kinds of activities should be multiplied from time to tome by taking further 'brain-storming' sessions.

3. The outcomes of the activities may be assessed in the real-life situations after organising the activities as described and discussed in the fourth chapter.

BIBLIOGRAPHY

Activity Report, Asian Disaster Preparedness Center (ADPC), Asian Institute of Technology, Bangkok, Thailand, 1992.

Alexander, David. "Natural Disasters: A Framework for Research and Teaching", *Disasters,* 1991, 15, 3, Sept, 209-226.

Alexander, David (1993). Natural Disasters, UCL Press London & Research Press New Delhi.

American Red Cross (1986). Chapter Activities in Disaster Community Education: A Resource Guide (ARC 4331). Emergency and Community Services, Research Development and Marketing: Washington DC.

Arya, A.S. "Action Plan for Earthquake Disaster Mitigation". In *Disaster Management,* Edited by V.K. Sharma, Indian Institute of Public Administration, New Delhi, 1995.

Ausubel, D.P. (1963). The Psychology of Meaningful Verbal Learning. Grune and Stratton: New York.

Ausubel, D.P. (1968). Educational Psychology: A Cognitive View. Holt, Rinehart and Winston: New York.

Baisden, B and Quarantelli, E.L., (1981). 'The Delivery of Mental Health Services in Community Disasters: An Outline of Research Findings', Journal of Community Psychology, 9, pp 195-203. In Richard Brook, *An Introduction To Disaster Theory for Social Workers.* Social Work Monographs, Norwich, 1990.

Bandura, A. and Walters, R. (1963). Social Learning and Personality Development. Holt, Rinehart and Winston: New York.

Bevli, U.K. et. al, (1981). Child Psychology- A Textbook for Class XII, NCERT, New Delhi.

Blaikie, Piers, Terry, Cannon & Ben, Wisner (1994). At Risk: Natural Hazards, People's Vulnerability and Disasters, Routledge, London.

Bloom, B.S., et al. (eds) 1956): Taxonomy of Educational Objectives, Handbook I, Cognitive Domain. Longman: London.

Bloom, B.S., Krathwohl, D.R., and Masia, B.B., (1956). Taxonomy of Educational Objectives, Handbook II, Affective Domain. Longman: London.

Brown, Barbara J. (1979). Disaster Preparedness and the United Nations Advance Planning for Disaster Relief, Published by UNITAR, Pergamon Press, New York.

Brown, Jennifer. "Evaluating Communications about Nuclear Energy: The Case Study of Sizewell –B" In *Hazards and the Communication of Risk,* Edited by John Handmer and Edmund Penning-Rowsell, Gower Publishing Company Limited, England, 1990.

Bruner, J.S. (1965). The Process of Education. Harvard University Press: Cambridge, Massachusetts.

Bruner, J.S. (1966). Towards a Theory of Instruction. Harvard University Press: Cambridge, Massachusetts.

Bruner, J.S. (1974). Beyond the Information Given. George Allen and Unwin: London.

Burke, J., et al., (1982). 'Changes in Children's Behaviour after a Natural Disaster', *American Journal of Psychiatry* 139:8, pp 1010-14 In Richard Brook, *An Introduction To Disaster Theory for Social Workers*. Social Work Monographs, Norwich, 1990.

Burton, Ian, et al. (1978). The Environment as Hazard, Oxford University Press, New York.

Carter, W. Nick. (1992). Disaster Management – A Disaster Manager's Handbook, Asian Development Bank, Philippines.

Chaudhari, B.R. "Emergencies: Perspectives and Strategies in the context of IDNDR". In *Natural Disaster Reduction for Nineties: Perspectives, Aspects and Strategies,* Edited by Prof. D.K. Sinha, International Journal Services, (Publications Division) Calcútta, 1992.

Cuny, Frederick. C. (1983). Disasters and Development, Oxford University Press.

Das, H.N. "Behavioural Aspects and Disaster Management". In *Natural Disaster Reduction – South Asian Regional Report,* Presented to The World Conference on the International Decade for Natural Disaster Reduction (IDNDR), Yokohama, Japan, May 23-27, 1994.

Davies, Anne, and Muir, Lynne (1984). 'Working with Volunteers and Self-help groups', in OLSEN, M.R., *Social Work and Mental Work* London: Tavistock. In Richard Brook, An Introduction to Disaster Theory for Social Workers. Social Work Monographs, Norwich, 1990.

Development of Modules for Training on Integrated Approach to Disaster Management and Regional/Rural Development Planning, Vol.I Report and Summary of Proceedings of the UNCRD – CIRDAP Workshop and Seminar on Development of Modules for Training on Disaster management, Dhaka, Bangladesh, 25-30 January, 1992. A finding on P.88.

Development of Modules for Training on Integrated Approach to Disaster Management and Regional/Rural Development Planning, Vol.II Report and Summary of Proceedings of the UNCRD – CIRDAP Workshop and Seminar on Development of Modules for Training on Disaster Management, Dhaka, Bangladesh, 25-30 January, 1992.

Directory of Voluntary Organisations, 1993. Council for Advancement of People's Action and Rural Technology (CAPART), New Delhi.

Disaster Management, Joint Assistance Centre, Gurgaon, Haryana. Vol. 4, 1984.

Disaster Management, Joint Assistance Centre, Gurgaon, Haryana. Vol. 2, 1982.

Disaster Management and Regional Development Planning with People's Participation. Vol. 1. United Nations Centre for

Regional Development, Nagoya, Japan and Centre on Integrated Rural Development for Asia and the Pacific, Bangladesh, 28 January – 1 February 1990, Dhaka, Bangladesh.

Disaster Mitigation in Asia and the Pacific: Seminar on the Regional Disaster Mitigation, Asian Development Bank, Philippines, 1991.

Down To Earth, Society for Environmental Communications, New Delhi. Vol. 3 No. 7, August 31, 1994.

Down To Earth, Society for Environmental Communications, New Delhi Vol. 6 No. 11, October 31, 1997.

Faupel, Charles E., Kelly, Susan P. & Petee, Thomas. "The Impact of Disaster Education on Household Preparedness for Hurricane Hugo", *International Journal of Mass Emergencies and Disasters,* 1992, 10, 1 Mar, 5-24.

Earthquake Preparedness 101. Planning Guidelines for Colleges and Universities, ED367263, 1992.

Emergency/Disaster Planning for Principals, 2nd edn. Natural Disasters Organisation, Canberra, 1992.

Filderman, Lynne. "Designing Public Education Programmes: A Current Perspective". In *Hazards and the Communication of Risk,* Edited by John Handmer and Edmund Penning-Rowsell, Gower Publishing Company Limited, England, 1990.

Friere, P. (1972): Pedagogy of the Oppressed. Penguin. Harmondsworth: Middlesex.

Ganguly, B. (1993). Education of Fight Against Natural Disasters. In *Natural Disaster Reduction,* Edited by G.K. Misra and G.C. Mathur, Reliance Publishing House & Indian Institute of Public Administration, New Delhi.

Gardiner, John. "Promoting a Risk Reduction Project: Experience in Thames Water". In *Hazards and the Communication of Risk,* Edited by John Handmer and Edmund Penning-Rowsell, Gower Publishing Company Limited, England, 1990.

Garrett, H.E. and Woodworth, R.S. (1985). Statistics in Psychology and Education. Vakils, Feffer and Simons, Ltd. Bombay.

Gautam, Ashutosh (1994). Earthquake - A Natural Disaster, Ashish Publishing House, New Delhi.

General Report on Landslides, by P. Jaganatha Rao, Symposium on Preparedness, Mitigation and Management of Natural Disaster, New Delhi, 1989, Vol.2.

General Studies Manual, For UPSC Civil Services Preliminary Examination, Tata Mc Graw-Hill Publishing Company Ltd., New Delhi, 1998.

Goutam, P.R. "Integrated Approach to Flood Disaster Management and Training Module for Hill Areas of Nepal". In *Development of Modules for Training on Integrated Approach to Disaster Management and Regional/Rural Development Planning,* Vol.II Report and Summary of Proceedings of the UNCRD -CIRDAP Workshop and Seminar on Development of Modules for Training on Disaster Management, Dhaka, Bangladesh, 25-30 January, 1992.

Handmer, John and Edmund Penning-Rowsell. "Is Succ- s Achievable" . In Hazards and the Communication of Risk, Edited by John Handmer and Edmund Penning-Rowsell, Gower Publishing Company Limited, England, 1990.

Harrison, Wendy (1987c). 'Report on the Working Group for Children or Young people affected by the Bradford City fire', Bradford Social Services. In Richard Brook, *An Introduction To Disaster Theory for Social Workers.* Social Work Monographs, Norwich, 1990.

Hazards, Disasters and Survival - A Booklet for Schools and the Community, Natural Disasters Organisation, Commonwealth of Australia 1992.

Hazard-wise, Emergency Management Australia. Classroom Resources for Teachers on Natural Hazards and Disasters. Ed. Chris Dolan, An Australian Disaster Awareness Project for the International Decade for Natural disaster Reduction, 1995.

Heller Robert W., et al., Disaster Controversy - Are You Prepared for the Worst? In Executive Educator, Vol. 13, No. 3, pp. 20-23 March, 1991.

Hornby, A.S. (1996). Oxford Advanced Learner's Dictionary of Current English, Fifth Edition, Ed. Jonathan Crowther, Oxford University Press, Oxford.

Hurlock, Elizabeth E. (1994). Child Growth and Development, Fifth Edition, Tata McGraw-Hill Publishing Company Ltd. New Delhi.

Illinois Department of Transportation –IDT (1980). Notifying Floodplain Residents: an Assessment of the Literature. Division of Water Resources: Chicago.

India Detailed National Report, World Conference on Disaster Reduction, Yokohama, Japan, May 23-27, 1994.

International Decade for Natural Disaster Reduction, Fact Sheet Series, No.1, Issued for: International Day for Natural Disaster Reduction, 11 October, 1995.

Jaiswal, N.K. and Kolte, N.V. (1981) Development of Drought-prone Areas, National Institute of Rural Development. Hyderabad.

Jeggle, Terry-Asian Institute of Technology, Bangkok, Thailand. Review, January, 1994.

Jingshen, Lu, Gangjian, Du & Gang, Song. "The Experience, Lesson and Reform of China's Disaster Management", *International Journal of Mass Emergencies and Disasters*, 1992, 10, 2, Aug, 315-327.

Joanne, M. Nigg, Director & Professor, Disaster Research Center, Newark, Delaware 19716-2581, (A personal letter dated 23 February, 1994).

Joy of Learning-Handbook of Environmental Education Activities. Centre for Environment Education, Ahmedabad, 1986.

Klingman, Alvidor (1988). 'School Community in Disaster Planning for Intervention', *Journal of Community Psychology* 16, pp. 205-15.

In Richard Brook, An Introduction To Disaster Theory for Social Workers. Social Work Monographs, Morwich, 1990.

Knowles, M.S. (1970). The Modern Practice of Adult Education. Associated Press: New York.

Knowles, M.S. (1984). The Adult Learner: a Neglected Species. (3rd Edn), Gulf: Houston.

Kulkarni, S.N. (1990). Famines, Droughts and Scarcities in India (Relief Measures and Policies), Chugh Publications, Allahabad.

Lunn, John, G. "Counter-Disaster/Emergency Planning in Tasmania", International Journal of Mass Emergencies and Disasters, 1990, 8, 2, Aug, 151-156.

Lystad, M. (1987). Human problems in major disasters: a training curriculum for emergency medical personnel. Rockville, Maryland: US Alcohol, Drug Abuse and Mental Health Administration.

Marks, David. "Imagery, Information and Risk". In Hazards and the Communication of Risk, Edited by John Handmer and Edmund Penning-Rowsell, Gower Publishing Company Limited, England, 1990.

Wilson, Colin. "Education and Risk". In Hazards and the Communication of Risk, Edited by John Handmer and Edmund Penning-Rowsell, Gower Publishing Company Limited, England, 1990.

Maureen O' Hagan & Maureen Smith (1990). Special Issues in Child Care. Brailliere Tindall, London.

Medina Jose Jr. "Training on Emergency and Post Emergency Responses and Measures to Cyclone/Typhoon Disaster including People's Participation". In *Development of Modules for Training on Integrated Approach to Disaster Management and Regional/Rural Development Planning,* Vol. II Report and Summary of Proceedings of the UNCRD – CIRDAP Workshop and Seminar on Development of Modules for Training on Disaster management, Dhaka, Bangladesh, 25-3 January, 1992.

Michaelis, A.R. "Inter-disciplinary Disaster Research". In *Natural Disaster Reduction for Nineties: Perspectives,*

Aspects & Strategies, Edited by Prof. D.K. Sinha, International Journal Services, (Publications Division) Calcutta, 1992.

Natural Disaster Reduction – South Asian Regional report, Presented to The World Conference on the International Decade for Natural Disaster Reduction (IDNDR), Yokohama, Japan, May 23-27, 1994.

Organisation of American States (OAS) (1984). Integrated Regional Development Planning: Guidelines and Case Studies from OAS Experience. OAS Development of Regional Development and Secretariat for Economic and Social Studies: Washington DC.

Ornstein, Allan C. & Francis P. Hunkins (1988). Curriculum – Foundations, Principles and Issues, Prentice Hall, Englewood Cliffs, New Jersey.

Pasrija, V.P. "Natural Disaster Management in India". In *Disaster Mitigation in Asia and the Pacific: Seminar on the Regional Disaster Mitigation,* Asian Development Bank, Philippines, 1991.

Perry Jr, J.B. & D.P. Meredith (1978). Collective Behaviour Response to Social Stress. St Paul, Minnesota: West.

Pickering, Kevin, T. & Owen, Lewis, A. (1994). An Introduction to Global Environmental Issues, Routledge, London.

Portis Mary & Richard Portis, Ready for Anything, In American School Board Journal, Vol. 178 No.11, 41-43pp, November, 1992.

Powell, B. and Penwick, E. (1983). 'Psychological distress following a natural disaster: a one-year follow-up of 98 flood victims', *Journal of Community Psychology* II, pp. 269-276. In Richard Brook, *An Introduction To Disaster Theory for Social Workers.* Social Work Monographs, Norwich, 1990.

Prescott, Daniel, A. (1957). The Child in the Educative Process, Nc Graw Hill Book Inc., New York.

Quarantelli, E.L. comment on a paper. In Disaster Management and Regional Development Planning with

People's Participation. Vol.1. United Nations Centre for Regional Development, Nagoya, Japan and Centre on Integrated Rural Development for Asia and the Pacific, Bangladesh, 28 January -1 February 1990, Dhaka, Bangladesh.

Rao, Jagannatha, P. "Mitigation of Landslide and Avalanche Hazards". In *Natural Disaster Reduction – South Asian Regional Report,* Presented to The World Conference on The International Decade for Natural Disaster Reduction (IDNDR), Yokohama, Japan, May 23-27, 1994.

Raphel B. (1983). The Anatomy of Bereavement, New York: Basic Books.

Recommendations for Emergency Management Planning for school Facilities, ED 384130, 1992.

Rogers, C.R. (1951). Client-Centred Therapy. Houghton Mifflin: Boston.

Rogers, C.R. (1969). Freedom To Learn. Charles E. Merrill, Columbus: Ohio.

Sapir, Debarati G. & Panaccione, Virginia C. "Health Sector Implications of the 1988 Earthquake in Yunnan Province, China", *Disasters,* 1992, 16, 2, June, 145-151.

Saunders, C.S. (1993). Safe at School: Awareness and Action for Parents of Kids Grades K-12, ED374193.

Sheehan, L. and Hewitt, K. (1969). A Pilot Survey of Global Natural Disasters of the Past Twenty Years. Working paper no.11. Institute of Behavioural Science, University of Colorado, Boulder.

Singh, D.P. "Managing Natural Disasters: The Role of Training." In *Natural Disaster Reduction for Nineties: Perspectives, Aspects and Strategies,* Edited by Prof. D.K. Sinha, International Journal Services, (Publications Division), Calcutta, 1992.

Sinha, D.K. "Coping with Natural Disasters: An Integrated Approach." In *Natural Disaster Reduction for Nineties: Perspectives, Aspects and Strategies,* Edited by Prof. D.K.

Sinha, International Journal Services, (Publications Division) Calcutta, 1992.

Siporin, Max (1976). 'Altruism, Disaster and Crisis Intervention'.

In Parad, Resnik, Parad (Eds.) *Emergency and Disaster Management* Bowie, Maryland. Charles Press. In Richard Brook, An *Introduction to Disaster Theory for Social Workers.* Social Work Monographs, Norwich, 1990.

Smithson, Michael: "Ignorance and Disasters", *International Journal of Mass Emergencies and Disasters,* 1990, 8, 3, Nov, 207-235.

State of India's Environment – A Citizen's Report, Floods, Flood Plains and Environmental Myths, Edited by Anil Agarwak & Sunita Narain, Centre for Science and Environment, New Delhi, 1991.

Stop Disasters Publication, *The Quarterly Magazine for IDNDR,* 1995 International Decade for Natural Disaster Reduction Secretariat, UN Department of Humanitarian Affairs, Palais des Nations, Geneva, Switzerland.

Stranks, Jeremy, W. (1991). The Handbook of Health & Safety Practice. Pitman, London.

Tatsch, J.H. (1977). Earthquakes: Cause, Prediction and Control, Tatsch Associates, Sudbury, Massachusetts, USA.

The Yokohama Strategy and Plan of Action for a Safer World – Guidelines for Natural Disaster Prevention, Preparedness and Mitigation. The World Conference on the International Decade for Natural Disaster Reduction (IDNDR), Yokohama, Japan, May 23-27, 1994.

The National Workshop on 'Role of Education and Training in Natural Disaster management' in Indian Adult Education Association, Newsletter, Vol. 20, No. 5, Aug, 1998, New Delhi.

Tiruvengadachari, S. "Space Technology for Hazard Monitoring, Forecasting & Warning". In *Natural Disaster Reduction – South Asian Regional Report,* Presented to

The World Conference on The International Decade for Natural Disaster Reduction (IDNDR), Yokohama, Japan, May 23-27, 1994.

Valussi, G. (1984). The Perception of Hazards in Geographical Education: Research Methods. in Graves, N.J. (ed), Research and Research Methods in Geographical Education. University of London Institute of Education: London.

Weirsing, K. (1995). Basic Principles and Elements of Disaster Mitigation. In Disaster Management. Edited by V.K. Sharma, National Center for Disaster Management, Indian Institute of Public Administration, New Delhi.

Wenger, Dennis (1978). 'Community Response to Disaster: Functional and Structural Alternations'. In Quarantelli (Ed.) Disasters: Theory and Research, London: Sage.. In Richard Brook, *An Introduction To Disaster Theory for Social Workers*. Social Work Monographs, Norwich, 1990.

Whittow, John (1980). Disasters: The Anatomy of Environmental Hazards Penguin Books, Harmondsworth.

World Disaster Report, 1997. Edited by Nick Cater and Peter Walker, International Federation of Red Cross and Red Crescent Societies, Switzerland.

INDEX

□□□